Words of Inspiration

✦

A Self-Divination and Healing Method for Awakening your Spiritual-Intuitive Side Using Playing Cards

Todd Jay Leonard

iUniverse, Inc.
New York Lincoln Shanghai

Words of Inspiration
A Self-Divination and Healing Method for Awakening your Spiritual-Intuitive Side Using Playing Cards

iUniverse, Inc.

For information address:
iUniverse, Inc.
2021 Pine Lake Road, Suite 100
Lincoln, NE 68512
www.iuniverse.com

ISBN: 0-595-29331-X

Printed in the United States of America

To my friend and mentor,

The Reverend Sarah Brown

Contents

Acknowledgements

First and foremost, I would like to offer my heartfelt thanks, with sincere devotion, to Talywala for all of her insightful and loving guidance she unfailingly offers to me on a regular and consistent basis. For this book in particular, as I sat with pen and paper in hand, the words would always seem to flow like a fast moving river; the divine light of her spirit and essence, coupled with her inspirational wisdom and spiritual balance, served as a beacon to me as I wrote the manuscript for this book. Her constant presence and selfless assistance was, and is, most welcomed and appreciated.

In addition, I wish to publicly acknowledge a number of earth-bound people who also assisted me in honing the written words and in utilizing my method of self-divination on a daily basis. I am greatly indebted to Chris Wissing, Cynthia Eiler, and Eriko Wilkinson who all diligently used my method, strongly urging me to publish formally my method of self-divination into a book. Thank you, dear friends, for your support and relentless insistence.

Conversations with a number of my colleagues, family, and friends also helped me to further develop the spiritual themes contained herein, as well as to define my thinking while putting this book together. I wish to acknowledge all of those who read parts or all of this manuscript, sparing me from inaccuracies in detail and oversights in assessment. Of course while they accept no responsibility for any defects, I am confident that their insightful suggestions and loving criticisms have made these word-delineations comparatively better. My sincere thanks to Shingo Ono, Mary Anderson, Craig Cameron Jean Straber, Alison Siemon, Mary Fidler, Claudette Bouchard, Kara Yamaguchi, William Fedchuk, and The Reverend Sarah Brown is an obligation I am most happy to fulfill.

To all of these I extend my heartfelt gratitude, enveloped in love and healing.

Introduction

Everyone, at some time or other in their life's journey, can use some assistance in focusing their energy in a positive, worthwhile direction. The majority of the time, people can do this instinctively by using their own judgment. It's during the odd times that we need a gentle nudge to help us begin the process of connecting more deeply to our spiritual side, or higher essence.

This process first involves recognizing the issue, then concentrating upon it in a loving way, and then finally addressing fully the area of our life that needs healing...or rejoicing! Our busy lives sometimes deny us the pleasure of realizing the bountiful blessings which shower us everyday; at times we need a warmhearted prompting to remind us of all the good that our lives bring to us.

In addition, it is sometimes difficult to see clearly issues or matters when so closely entwined with them. A loving reminder of an aspect that we may not be aware exists; are avoiding subconsciously; or are too busy to address properly, may be all that is needed to direct positive energy toward it, in order to help us continue steadily on our life's journey.

Words of Inspiration: A Self-Divination and Healing Method for Awakening your Spiritual-Intuitive Side Using Playing Cards is a method of self-divination which utilizes ordinary playing cards along with this book. When used together, this method can act as a "jump start" for inspiration or guidance at the times in your life when some healing direction is needed.

A regular deck of ordinary playing cards (52 cards with the four suits—*hearts, clubs, diamonds,* and *spades*) is all that is needed to intuit an individual reading for yourself. Each ordinary playing card has been matched to either a Red Suit or a Black Suit reading for the 26 "key-words" that are individually delineated alphabetically in this book.

This book outlines the keywords using five stages: first, the intuited word is explained in a thoughtful essay that offers you, the reader, an initial introduction to the word for concentrated reflection. Second, a reading of the keyword's Red Suit position is given. Third, a reading of the keyword's Black Suit position is given. Fourth, an intention, which offers love and healing to the situation or aspect that needs attention and/or is related to your everyday life and interactions, is offered. And finally, questions to guide you in your own self-healing are listed.

Everyone and everything is made up of energy. The universal life-force energy that pervades all is a part of what and who we are. Whether you have a casual idea of "energy," or you are directly connected to "energy" through energy-based therapies, you will be able to access your God-given magnetic field of energy simply by concentrating and focusing upon utilizing it in a positive, healing way.

Getting in touch with your "energetic" side will help you progress more quickly on your own individual spiritual journey. Learning to tap into your personal, limitless energy field will also inspire you and allow you the freedom to become more intuitively aware of the happenings occurring around you—and to trust that intuition more readily. It will help you to recognize more deeply and clearly the importance behind the various people with whom your path crosses on a daily basis. In essence, life is one long learning experience. There are no accidents, only lessons to be learned and understood.

How to Use the Cards

A good way to begin is to sit quietly on the floor or in a comfortable chair with your eyes closed. Slowly, but deliberately, breathe deeply to open your energy centers that align your body from the top of your head to the base of your spine. Do this until you feel calm and relaxed.

Next, hold your hands with your palms facing one another, slightly cupped, and about five inches apart. Concentrate on the energy that is contained between your hands. After approximately 1 minute, you will begin to feel the energy from your own magnetic field strongly between your hands. Gently push the energy that is between your hands by moving them in a gentle back and forth motion. Feel the energy pulsing between them. Once you feel this sensation, begin to play with the energy by rolling it like an invisible ball or by widening your hands to allow the energy to extend. There is virtually no limit to how far the energy can be elongated. Have fun with it!

This simple exercise demonstrates quite clearly that you do indeed have *ki* or *chi* (the Japanese and Chinese words for "universal life-force energy"). We all have it. We can all access it. We can all benefit from it. Once you feel this strong connection to the energy-source, take the deck of playing cards into your hands and hold them. This helps to make the cards *yours* by allowing your healing energy to penetrate the cards thoroughly. It is best to have a special deck of cards that you only use for this purpose.

Manipulate or shuffle the cards in any manner to further permit your life-force energy to saturate the cards completely. Intuitively, you will feel and know when it is enough.

Finally, with your hand on the deck, spread the cards in a long straight line (similar to that of a dealer in a casino). The cards may overlap, but each should be easily visible.

Continue to maintain your focus and concentration; be mindful of your own energy. Move the palm of your dominant hand (facedown) over the length of the cards. Be aware of any shift in energy or sensation you may feel in your hand as it moves. Go back to the area(s) where you felt the strongest sensation. When you intuitively feel you have reached a card that is calling you, select it. This card corresponds to either a *Red Suit* or *Black Suit* position of a keyword listed in this book (which is the target area of healing you need to focus upon or acknowledge at that moment).

Please don't be discouraged if you don't feel any strong sensation in the beginning. The energy is there—it just needs to be fine-tuned, built up, and strengthened. If you feel this way, whatever card you choose will still be intuitively selected and will offer you the same benefit of an insightful reading. Also, know that your spirit guides, your angels, and your higher self will be guiding your hands to choose the most appropriate card for your current needs.

Some people decide never to select cards by sensing with their own magnetic energy field, but instead opt to allow their angels, spirit guardians, and/or higher self to aid them in intuitively selecting the card that is best for them at that moment.

Others choose to use a combination of both—the energetic, tingling sensation generated in their hand *and* their higher selves—to select the most appropriate card for them. Still, some people opt to only use their life-force energy to feel, in a physical sense, which card is best for them. The most important point to remember, and one of the beautiful parts about using this book with playing cards, is that there is no right or wrong way to seek guidance from them. Any manner *you* choose to intuit a card will be the right way, at that moment.

Each of us, as we progress on our individual journeys, constantly discriminates between methods and techniques in order to choose the most appropriate way of gaining guidance for our own particular needs. All of us have personal preferences regarding spiritual guidance that differ from others. The ultimate goal, however, is very much the same—to connect with the Divine that is present within us all. It is necessary that *you* feel comfortable and at ease with the manner in which you choose to intuit the cards. Mixing and matching through experiential means will allow you to decide upon a style that is consoling and agreeable to you and your wishes. Experiment and explore all the possibilities of the cards that await you. Perhaps you will discover a way which will be guided by your own personal essence and being, certainly making it uniquely yours!

If by chance you feel energy emanating from two or more cards, perhaps this is a message from the Universe to select them all. When combined, they could offer more pointed insight and more accurately reveal issues or aspects that you are in need of addressing…or in rejoicing!

After selecting a card (or cards), it is a good idea to hold the card cupped in your hands (or in a prayer position between your hands), allowing your energy to penetrate it completely and to mix with the loving, healing energy generated by the card. Using the key ("List of Cards and Corresponding Words") following this introduction, focus and concentrate on the intuitively chosen word for several minutes. What thoughts or images come to your mind? Does anyone or anything in particular pop up without warning? As you focus on the card, note any visual images that appear in your mind's eye (or "third-eye," the energy center located on your lower forehead, between your eyes).

It is a good idea to have a pen and some paper handy in order to write down any insights, sensations, visions, images or messages you hear, see, feel or intuit. Many wonderfully inspired thoughts could shower your mind's eye, so you need to be prepared. Each and every insight will have significance. The *raison d'etre* may not present itself immediately, but eventually it will become clear to you. Don't worry if you cannot write down everything (or you consciously choose not to interrupt your intuited visions with the added distraction of writing). You will remember what you need to remember when you need to remember it. All is stored for future retrieval in your vast memory bank. God has a miraculous way of allowing you to call up specific information in order to integrate and focus it into your being, at the appropriate time that is best for you and your needs, and in the moment when you most need it.

When you choose the card initially, it will either be a Red Suit or Black Suit playing card. This is useful when reading about the keyword and your intention for that particular card. In this book, look up the card in the "List of Cards and Corresponding Words" (each card is listed in numerical order from the *Ace* to the *King;* from hearts, to clubs, to diamonds, to spades); the healing words are listed alphabetically in this book. First, read the insightful essay about the word. Then read the "position" (*Red Suit* or *Black Suit*) of your selected card.

Included with each delineated word is an intention that you can say aloud or silently, three times. It is important to make your intention to the Universe clear. If the urge hits you, shout it out! Never take an intention lightly, because as you make it, the process is set into motion for it to be acted upon. The old saying, "be careful what you wish for," has substance and meaning. Thoughts, intentions, and affirmations should be sent forth deliberately, carefully and lovingly. Even off-the-cuff comments or wishes can become reality, as the Universe doesn't necessarily distinguish between casual and serious intentions so readily. God and the Universe, however, more readily act upon intentions that are made in clear and unambiguous terms, from the heart, and with love and healing.

As a reflective exercise, each word lists four questions that can aid you in your self-healing. Read each one slowly and take a moment to meditate upon it in order to really process the intent behind your answer. Thoughts that just "pop" into your head are not accidental, but divinely guided suggestions to help you understand why you intuitively chose the card you did. Reflect positively. Reflect lovingly. Reflect deliberately. And above all, reflect honestly. Ultimately, self-reflection will aid you tremendously on your journey and in understanding your life experiences, personal feelings, everyday interactions, private relationships, and your divine purpose in life.

Points to Ponder

It is important to open your mind to the possibility that the intuited position of the word may or may not be directly related to your own situation or condition. It could be referring to someone related to you in the peripheral edges of your life. Perhaps it is a message for a loved one, a friend...or even a foe. You may very well be the messenger or earth angel chosen to pass along the intuited information. God works in mysterious ways. Often, the process is as important as the result.

For instance, drawing the card that correlates with the keyword "Charity" may not refer to you not being charitable to someone else, but may be in reference to someone who has behaved uncharitably towards you. By focusing intently on the card, a clear meaning will most likely appear to you. Or perhaps you have been conducting yourself in a charitable manner and are being commended for your good deeds—a spiritual pat on the back, of sorts.

Only you know the intent behind the intuited card and position of the word's meaning. Your own interpretation, coupled with your intuition or "gut feeling" will reveal how you should be reacting to that particular word at that exact moment. Often we tend to outwardly act in a certain manner or say certain things, but inwardly we know in our hearts what is sincere and what is not. The card you choose may be nudging you in a spiritual way to deal with or reflect upon an attitude, situation, feeling, emotion or idea that you have been avoiding. Concentrate upon the card and the essay connected to the card deeply. Again, much will be revealed to you, as you offer love and healing to the word and situation that prompted the selection of that card. Remember, there are no accidents. The Universe, with the divine intervention and help of our all-loving God, has guided you to that card for a reason. Search from within for the answer to the purpose. It is there.

In addition, a pleasant aspect of this method of divination is that the word doesn't necessarily focus upon a situation that needs improving or addressing, as much as acknowledgment and acceptance. It is important to look at each card you draw in a loving light, pulling out the positive, life-giving energy generated in it. Do not focus upon any potentially negative aspects of the word unless it is only to admit and acknowledge, conquer, and finally release it. Never dwell unnecessarily upon any negatively generated feelings or energy. It's not worth it in the whole scheme of things. However, the intuited word could be serving as a wake-up call, like cold water thrown on your face. It could force you to admit, conquer and release the bad habit, poor attitude or false idea you may be harboring with regards to how you have been progressing on your life's journey. In this case, it is good to address the negativity in order to release it and find closure with it.

Remember, we all have a "soul in progress." That is the whole reason why we are here at this point in time—to learn and to move forward so that our soul can progress on its most wonderful journey. In closing, I offer you, dear fellow journeyer, this intention from my heart:

"Godspeed and God bless you as you continue on your joyous journey, in search of and in fulfilling your unique life's purpose. I offer you this intention with love and healing."

List of Words and Corresponding Cards

Suits of Hearts and Clubs

ABUNDANCE	Red: *Ace of Hearts*	Black: *Ace of Clubs*
ACCEPTANCE	Red: *Two of Hearts*	Black: *Two of Clubs*
BLISS	Red: *Three of Hearts*	Black: *Three of Clubs*
CHARITY	Red: *Four of Hearts*	Black: *Four of Clubs*
COMPASSION	Red: *Five of Hearts*	Black: *Five of Clubs*
COURAGE	Red: *Six of Hearts*	Black: *Six of Clubs*
CREATIVITY	Red: *Seven of Hearts*	Black: *Seven of Clubs*
DEVOTION	Red: *Eight of Hearts*	Black: *Eight of Clubs*
EMPOWER	Red: *Nine of Hearts*	Black: *Nine of Clubs*
ENLIGHTENMENT	Red: *Ten of Hearts*	Black: *Ten of Clubs*
FAITH	Red: *Jack of Hearts*	Black: *Jack of Clubs*
FORGIVENESS	Red: *Queen of Hearts*	Black: *Queen of Clubs*
HOPE	Red: *King of Hearts*	Black: *King of Clubs*

Suits of Diamonds and Spades

INSPIRATION	Red: *Ace of Diamonds*	Black: *Ace of Spades*
JOY	Red: *Two of Diamonds*	Black: *Two of Spades*
KNOWLEDGE	Red: *Three of Diamonds*	Black: *Three of Spades*
LOVE	Red: *Four of Diamonds*	Black: *Four of Spades*
PEACE	Red: *Five of Diamonds*	Black: *Five of Spades*
PRAYER	Red: *Six of Diamonds*	Black: *Six of Spades*
PROMISE	Red: *Seven of Diamonds*	Black: *Seven of Spades*
RESPECT	Red: *Eight of Diamonds*	Black: *Eight of Spades*
TOLERANCE	Red: *Nine of Diamonds*	Black: *Nine of Spades*
TRUTH	Red: *Ten of Diamonds*	Black: *Ten of Spades*
UNDERSTANDING	Red: *Jack of Diamonds*	Black: *Jack of Spades*
WORTHINESS	Red: *Queen of Diamonds*	Black: *Queen of Spades*
ZEST	Red: *King of Diamonds*	Black: *King of Spades*

Abundance

Living a life full of *abundance* is a God-given right that each of us possesses. The Universe makes possible an infinite supply of abundance that is benevolent and affluent, not only in terms of "things" or the amount one has in the bank, but also in reference to what is available on a spiritual, emotional, and physical level. Reaping the fullness of all that is rightfully yours is an entitlement guaranteed to you by the Universe.

If you are not currently living your life abundantly, then you should begin to do so immediately. The copious supply, which is all around us, is yours for the asking. In order for you to attract abundance, it may entail changing an untrue deep-rooted personal belief you may be harboring ("I'm not worthy..."); an attitude of denial ("I don't deserve it..."); or an ingrained idea ("My parents never had anything and were poor, so I'll never have anything and will always be poor...").

Defining in your heart what constitutes abundance to make *you* happy will aid you in acquiring more than you'll ever need spiritually, emotionally, physically, and economically. The first step is to erase any negative language you are thinking, believing, or saying out loud (I won't...; I can't...; I don't...) and replace it with positive vibratory messages to the Universe (I am...; I do...; I can...).

If by chance you are living an abundant life at this moment, then congratulations on your achievement. You learned the secret to life's lesson of living life in the positive—*ask and ye shall receive*—and are enjoying the wonderful benefits of doing so. If you are not living an abundant life, then what are you waiting for? Get on with it.

Red Suit *(Ace of Hearts)*

Splendid. You are being recognized by Spirit for your ability to savor what is available to you. Often people only think of "abundance" as relating to what material possessions one has, and in financial, monetary terms. Of course, these are significant and are included in the definition of "abundance," but they are not the only things that constitute this rich word. Abundance also means living abundantly by enjoying all the Universe has to offer; having spiritual abundance by forging a personal relationship with the Creator; and emotional abundance borne out of love for a partner, parent, child, sibling or friend which is ultimately reflected back to you in kind and degree. By offering abundant affection to others, you receive it back reciprocally. Being in abundance involves a multi-faceted and leveled way of thinking and behaving. Possessing the proper attitude involves having positive thoughts, which in turn creates positive, life-enhancing energy. This *is* the best way to begin creating an abundant life…and in maintaining abundance indefinitely.

Take a moment to think about all the abundance you have in your life and be sincerely thankful for it. Giving thanks to God and the Universe, whether it be through praying, meditating, or living life in the positive is a necessary ingredient in perpetuating the positive cycle of creating, harnessing, and enjoying continued abundance of all kinds in your life.

Black Suit *(Ace of Clubs)*

Self-pity is a loathsome rut for a person to be in. Concentrating and obsessing upon what you don't have available to you in your life will only reinforce the vibratory messages you are sending out into the Universe, and in turn will only give back to you what you give—negativity. Sometimes people negatively focus their life-force energy by blaming others for their lot in life. Living life perpetually as a victim will drain you dry of all the energy you have, and will push the potential for abundance away. Anger, envy, jealousy, fear, and hatred allow you to wallow in a cesspool of self-pity ("Poor me..." or "Why me?").

Your happiness is not dependent upon the attitude of others. Your abundance is not dependent upon the actions of others. You, and only you, are responsible for your feelings and actions. In order for you to grow spiritually and to have an excess of abundance in your life, you must search within yourself to find it in your heart 1) to forgive; 2) to release; and 3) to go onward in order to become abundantly happy, abundantly secure financially, and abundantly connected to the Divine which is in you.

The first step is to pinpoint clearly what is blocking your ability to have what you want, to be what you want, and to live the life you want in abundance. Next, understand the blockage. Go back into that deeply-rooted wound and face it head on. Then release the negative energy associated with it completely. Ultimately, find it in your heart to forgive.

It is vital to transfer all the energy that is being expended on negatively generated emotions and focus it more clearly. By going higher within yourself you can regain control of your destiny. This will help you move forward to fulfill your life's dreams and soul's desires. Once you clear the obstacles that are hindering you from achieving abundance in Spirit, in life, or in love, you will begin to realize the universal law of "positive creates positive."

You intuited this card in the Black Suit because there is something in your past, or in your life currently, that has you stuck. Reverse the cycle by reaching deep into yourself to find the cause of the problem that is hindering you from having abundance that is pure and loving; or from enjoying the abundance you already have. Seek it out and deal with it. You are entitled to an abundant life, which is not only personally enriching, but also spiritually uplifting, and financially secure. Shed your negative attitudes about relationships, money, and life. Exchange your indulgent self-pity for high self-esteem. You can do it if you truly want to. It is ultimately your choice.

Healing Intention

"I live abundantly in Spirit, reaping all the good that the Universe has at its disposal. I invite the loving and healing abundance of the Universe to manifest itself richly in my life. I live abundantly, having more than I will ever need. I have abundance in Spirit and relish all that the Universe makes available to me. I offer this intention with love and healing."

Reflective Questions for your Self-Healing

-Why did I choose the card in the position I did?
-What lesson can be learned by focusing on this card?
-How do I interpret the meaning of this card?
-Why is this card significant to me at this moment?

Acceptance

Acceptance is a concept that many would like to think they practice on a consistent, regular basis, but in fact have a difficult time in doing. By not accepting people or situations just because they do not fit into *your* idea of what "acceptable" is in this life experience, does not mean that what they are doing, feeling or choosing is necessarily wrong. It's just different.

When other peoples' ideas, behaviors or characters do not coincide with that of yours, it is very easy to discount them completely by saying, "I don't accept you, what you're doing, or how you behave." And ultimately it is your choice to do so. But, is it the best choice? In most instances, no one is asking you to agree categorically, but only to accept them for who they are, what they are, and as they are. Even someone you encounter on your journey, who seemingly has no redeeming social or spiritual value in your eyes, is still one of God's precious children and is traveling alongside you on your journey. These are not merely chance meetings. They are a part of life's many lessons.

Indeed, each of us has merit; each of us has value; and most importantly, each of us can offer one another guidance from which to learn. Your meeting a person or encountering a situation which tests your ability to accept unconditionally could be signaling a need for you to make amends in this life for a past digression. Often times we are strategically placed by the Universe in situations or in the company of people that test our level of acceptability. In these cases, we need to look beyond the obvious and go within to seek out the deeper meaning as to "why?"

If a person close to you is testing your acceptance level, perhaps you should sit down and reflect upon your attitudes to try to learn why this person (or situation) has presented itself to you and how you can grow from it. Offer acceptance to others who are traveling sincerely on their journeys, but who do not fit into your own idea of what they should be doing. It is not up to you to judge them, only to accept them by offering tolerance, respect and love.

Red Suit *(Two of Hearts)*

Accepting people for who they are and as they are is very important for our soul's progress. Accepting other people does not necessarily mean you agree with or understand them completely—it just means that you respect their decisions, good and bad, and accept them for who and what they are on this earthly plane. "Accepting" is more a matter of "lovingly acknowledging" another person.

You intuited this card in the Red Suit signaling that you have recently demonstrated the virtue of acceptance in some form—whether it was toward another brother or sister...or to *yourself.* Self-acceptance is just as vital for a soul's progress as is offering acceptance to another. At times, it is easier to accept others more readily than we can accept ourselves.

Perhaps you recently offered some advice in an accepting, loving way that encouraged a fellow journeyer. Maybe you chose to accept, rather than to reject, a fellow being with whom you came into contact but didn't clearly understand or agree with his/her attitudes or beliefs. The process of accepting or offering acceptance to others and to situations (which do not infringe upon your own sense of moral duty; or hinder you on your own individual progress of your life's journey), elevates your spiritual awareness. Your own progress is further aided by choosing not to judge unduly others with whom you encounter. No matter which particular reason applies, continue to be accepting of others and of yourself!

Black Suit *(Two of Clubs)*

God is quite savvy in creating a situation or placing people in our path at the right moment to help us to reflect upon our own lives, attitudes and priorities. The secret is to seize the opportunity and learn from it, rather than to fight, ignore, or deny the situation or person exists. When we are placed strategically in situations or with people who really test the fiber of our beings, it is important to remember that this is done in order for us to progress spiritually, emotionally and physically on our journey. These souls are sent to us by our angels to remind us of our place in the Universe.

The Black Suit of this card suggests that you are struggling with an issue which requires you to accept a situation, person, attitude, belief system, or an aspect of *yourself* which you are having trouble in accepting fully. Trying to manipulate a situation, to change a person, to abandon a situation, or to deny your true feelings is not the way to resolve this issue. Look deeply at the reasons why you have difficulty accepting the situation or person that precipitated your drawing this card in this position. You need to work slowly through your reservations to determine if you are justified in not offering acceptance with purity of motive; or if in fact you are more concerned with controlling the person or situation out of a need which is selfish or self-centered, rather than one which is borne out of love and healing. Some situations and people are not for us to control, but to accept. Offering understanding, which is filled with hope and love, will help to resolve the issue more satisfactorily than trying to manipulate it.

Perhaps this card refers to your having difficulty in accepting yourself fully. If this is the case, then concentrate upon the area in your life that is hard for you to accept and then release it completely. Often times we place tremendous obstacles in our life's path because we do not accept ourselves as we are, for what we are, and for who we are. We can certainly be our own worst enemy at times.

Only you know the exact person or situation to which this card refers. Abandoning a situation, refusing to accept another person's choices or denying yourself self-acceptance are not helping you on your journey. Go deep within to confront and then to purge the attitude, belief, idea or action that is not allowing you to be an accepting person…to others or to yourself.

Healing Intention

"I accept myself completely and unconditionally. I am accepting of people who cross my life's path. I accept situations that present themselves which may test my ability to accept, but which offer me a chance to learn and to grow spiritually, and emotionally. I offer acceptance which has purity of motive and which is non-judgmental. I offer this intention with love and healing."

Reflective Questions for your Self-Healing

-Why did I choose the card in the position I did?
-What lesson can be learned by focusing on this card?
-How do I interpret the meaning of this card?
-Why is this card significant to me at this moment?

Bliss

True *bliss* is a combination of happiness, joy, ecstasy, delight, rapture, glee, gladness…exhilaration. It is the highest happiness we humans experience on this earthly plane. Being blissful is enjoying life and Spirit fully and completely. Having bliss is being happy with who and what you are—your condition…your life.

The feeling of "bliss" is so powerful that it can rub off onto others who have the good fortune to find themselves in the presence of a truly blissful person. People who have bliss in their lives have auras that expand limitlessly into the Universe. These powerful energy fields, which emanate in all directions, collide and mix with the energies of the people with whom these blissful people meet.

It is no coincidence that when we meet such people that we too feel immediately uplifted from just being close to them. On an energy level, information regarding a person's emotional state has already been exchanged with all the other people's with whom they come into contact…even before seeing them physically or exchanging words or greetings with them!

When you encounter people who obviously have bliss in their lives, stand close to them and bask in the loving glow of this emotion; observe their energy and the happiness that they generate from it. Allow yourself to enjoy this feeling and then begin to work towards having this same bliss in your life. Once you achieve this emotional state, relish it with abandon. Ahh, bliss…what a wonderful and glorious feeling it is. Thank you, God, for giving us the capacity to enjoy this satisfying sensation.

Red Suit *(Three of Hearts)*

Aren't you the lucky one! You intuited this card in this position to remind you of the "bliss" you experience in your life. Scan your mind for any blissful recollections to which this card refers. Often times we get so caught up with life that we fail to stop to think about the things which make us blissful. Perhaps the Universe is hinting to you to pause momentarily to enjoy the bliss you have sprinkled about your presence.

The beautiful part about bliss, and having bliss, is that it can be something simple like a fond childhood memory, or a pleasing aroma that takes you back to a particular period in your life. It can also be a feeling you have for an accomplishment or a success you have achieved. Bliss can be related to a relationship you have with a family member, a significant other, or a friend.

Being full of bliss gives you a chance to share your happiness with others by spreading your blissful vibrations. It also allows you to rise above any potential negativity that might try to infiltrate your energy field.

Close your eyes, take a deep breath, and think long and hard about the bliss you experience in your life. Take a mental journey to a blissful place in your heart; saturate your mind with that luxurious feeling; allow it to permeate your entire being. Once you are there, bathe yourself in this God-given emotion that is full of love, joy, and happiness. If ever you feel your bliss waning, go back to that part of you that remembers bliss and recapture it. Go boldly, dear blissful journeyer, and continue harnessing all the bliss you can…as well as spreading it out to others.

Black Suit *(Three of Clubs)*

Sometimes we mortals get so caught up in the rat race of everyday life that when we are offered a chance to have bliss in our lives, we let it slip by without seizing it. Why do we do this?

Perhaps it isn't a conscious act, but nonetheless some of us find it preferable to be unhappy. As odd as it may sound, the familiarity of an unhappy situation is more appealing to that of a happy one. Strange? Yes. Uncommon? No.

The type of person who wallows in unhappiness considers the risk of trying to leave this joyless state greater than pursuing a happiness which may be fleeting. The person has convinced him/herself that the constancy of being unhappy is more comforting because it is familiar. This is largely because the end result of such feelings is well-known to the person and the emotions related to the sadness are anticipated beforehand (the idea of "being disappointed if one is not disappointed"). The fear of not being able to find happiness and bliss in the first place, and the anxiety created over not being able to hold onto it, propels a person void of bliss deeper into this damaging mindset.

Having bliss in your life doesn't have to be a fleeting moment in time, but an everyday reality. If one can choose to be *unhappy*, why can't one choose to be *happy*? It goes back to the idea of "is the glass half-full or is it half-empty?" A person experiencing bliss would immediately declare the glass "half-full" while a person who is not blissful would most likely see it as being "half-empty." Reversing a negative trend or attitude in your life that is holding you back from experiencing true bliss will allow you to welcome bliss back into your life.

Sometimes we fall into deep ruts because the situations and circumstances in them seem consistent in a familiar sort of way. True change is regarded as being "scary" and unfamiliar which keeps us from seeking to leave the strife that is being inflicted upon us in these instances. If you are currently denying yourself your own God-given right to enjoy a blissful life, then do something about it...and fast. If it requires you to remove yourself from a situation—then do it. If it means forgiving someone...or yourself—then do it.

You intuited this card because you are at odds with having and enjoying bliss in your life. Whatever life situation you find yourself in—no matter how bad you may think it is—there is hope. The secret is to rise above the negativity and release it; replace the void with positive, life-enhancing energy. Instead of avoiding or letting happiness pass you by, begin the process of seizing every opportunity that comes your way to bring bliss into your life…and then enjoy it. This may be the biggest favor you ever do for yourself.

Healing Intention

"I lead a life which is full of the energy-enhancing emotion of bliss. I allow bliss to permeate every cell of my body, every inch of my aura. The bliss I experience and enjoy spreads to others with whom I come into contact. I wish that by my example, they too may realize the bliss they have in their lives, but have failed to enjoy fully. I offer this intention with love and healing."

Reflective Questions for your Self-Healing

-Why did I choose the card in the position I did?
-What lesson can be learned from focusing on this card?
-How do I interpret the meaning of this card?
-Why is this card significant to me at this moment?

Charity

Charity, of course, is the act of giving money or help to someone in need. It can also be an organization that assists the poor or downtrodden. A more spiritual interpretation of this beautiful word, however, is the kindness or forgiveness a person demonstrates in judging others.

Conducting yourself in a charitable manner, even to those who are unkind to you, allows you to rise above the negative energy which is generated from the unkindness that is bestowed upon you. Being charitable, rather than vengeful, allows you to release the potential for anger or frustration. This consciously positive act will ultimately aid you in moving forward on your life's journey.

Red Suit *(Four of Hearts)*

The fact that you intuitively selected this card means the Universe is congratulating you on your good works. Perhaps recently you aided someone in need, or gave love and encouragement to a person who was in a desperate state of emotional, physical or mental distress. Maybe you took the high road and acted charitably toward someone who had insulted you or tried to hurt you in some way.

Think positively, while focusing your healing energy on this card; concentrate on all aspects of "charity" in a loving light—the act that precipitated your choosing this card may very well appear to you.

Black Suit *(Four of Clubs)*

Selecting this Black Suit card may mean that you have recently acted unkindly to a fellow being, or have been selfish in your interactions with others. What prompted the Universe to guide you to choose this card in this position? The situation or instance in which you may have been less than kind is in your heart. Pull it out. Face it head on. And let it go. Make a promise to yourself to be more charitable in the future.

Healing Intention

"I will only react charitably toward others so that they and I may be kinder, gentler people in the future. I strive to be charitable to all. I offer this intention with love and healing."

Reflective Questions for your Self-Healing

-Why did I choose the card in the position I did?
-What lesson can be learned by focusing on this card?
-How do I interpret the meaning of this card?
-Why is this card significant to me at this moment?

Compassion

Many people erroneously confuse the emotions of *compassion* and pity. What a huge mistake! "Pity" tends to suggest that there is some degree of regret or sorrow involved, where "compassion" conveys more of a feeling of hope, and even a desire to help alleviate the distress or suffering of the person or situation. So, pitying people or their situations is much different from feeling compassion for them, in a healing and loving way.

Possessing a sense or capacity to feel compassion for others is an essential ingredient in the recipe for world peace and understanding. Without it, we would be doomed as there would be no purpose to life as we know it. God gave us the gift to feel compassion for others in order to empathize in a sympathetic way with those who experience hardships or misfortunes of some kind. This ability helps us to share, support, and assist our brothers and sisters who have great difficulty on their journeys.

Compassion, which is filled with loving light, is a powerful force, second only to pure love. When we experience a sincere feeling of compassion, we send out positive vibrations into the Universe that are filled with love and hope. Compassion from the heart cleanses the soul. In the process, it helps us to empathize with others whom we come into contact while on our wonderful journeys. Possessing a feeling of compassion allows the Universe to teach us how to understand the many lessons life has in store for us.

Red Suit *(Five of Hearts)*

Dear, dear, compassionate soul! The Universe is recognizing you for your compassion. Perhaps recently you felt compassion from the heart for another, or you have offered a compassionate word or lent a compassionate ear to a troubled soul, which ultimately helped him/her to move forward on their journey. Your compassion was given lovingly and was accepted with a knowing appreciation. This positive act will come back to you one hundredfold.

Thoughts and attitudes, which are compassionate in nature, are just as important as actual words and deeds. Only you know with complete certainty if your intent is genuine when interacting with others, or if your attitude is true and authentic with how you are conducting yourself in your daily life.

Concentrate lovingly upon this card to help reveal what precipitated your choosing this particular word at this exact time. Gently lay your hands over your heart to allow your healing energy to envelop your compassionate heart. This will help to aid you in clearly focusing upon a particular person, situation or action. Go forth and continue being compassionate. It suits you.

Black Suit *(Five of Clubs)*

Possessing a sense of compassion is admirable—if it is not selfish and is pure. As mentioned in the essay, "pity" is sometimes mistaken for the feeling of loving compassion. They are not the same.

Compassion comes from the heart and can be felt all the way to the core of the soul. Pity, on the other hand, is more ego-based and is felt mentally rather than emotionally or spiritually. Offering someone pity places you in a superior position in which to look down upon him or her. True compassion does not.

Some people mistakenly believe, for example, that simply throwing money at a homeless person is an act of compassion. This is the easy way out. The intent behind the action is what distinguishes it from being a truly assisting, compassionate act…or from being a self-serving action of pity borne out of a feeling of superiority. Serving others, as well as offering love to all, is part of the reason why we are all here on this earthly plane. The service we offer to others must come from love and compassion that is sincere in order for it to count. In contrast, hiding behind pretenses, which outwardly appear to be compassionate in nature, but in fact are generated from ulterior motives that are done to impress others, or to satisfy a selfish need to feel superior, is not helping you on your journey. Compassion comes from the heart. Compassion is sincere. Compassion is enveloped with love.

You intuited this card because you have recently neglected a fellow journeyer by not being sufficiently compassionate or by not offering a compassionate word or ear in a time of need. Or conversely, you have been behaving compassionately for the wrong reasons which could be construed as being self-serving or borne out of a need to impress others by seeking approval of some sort, albeit falsely.

You know your true intent behind your interactions with others and the sincere attitude with which you are conducting yourself. Reassess these and change any false ideas you are harboring in the name of compassion. You are fooling no one but yourself. The Universe knows your true intent even if those around you do not. Look deep into this area of your life and distinguish between a feeling of pity and compassion. Once you compare them, you will never forget the difference. It will become clear.

<u>Healing Intention</u>

"I offer compassion to all those in need which is borne out of love and hope. I am compassionate in my interactions with others and with myself. I offer this intention with love and healing."

<u>Reflective Questions for your Self-Healing</u>

-Why did I choose the card in the position I did?
-What lesson can be learned by focusing on this card?
-How do I interpret the meaning of this card?
-Why is this card significant to me at this moment?

Courage

To follow one's own convictions takes moral *courage*. To deal with fear, anger, pain or danger takes personal courage. The power to conquer these life-obstacles comes from the quality of having courage.

Spiritual growth depends upon not only the ability to understand yourself more fully, but to have the courage to face directly the situations, beliefs, habits, attitudes, or people in your life that are hindering your progress on your journey. Choose not to let these outside forces keep you from moving forward. No one can help you better than you can help yourself. From within, you can change yourself; you can recreate yourself to be a more powerful, courageous, and spiritual being.

Each of us regards differently what constitutes courage. To one person, the mere act of getting on an airplane may require him/her to muster all the courage possible to do what millions of other people do on a daily basis. For another, confronting a personal demon that has been a monkey on his/her back for years may be the single most courageous act s/he will ever perform. So, the "act" of courage is not nearly as important as the emotions and feelings related to it. What may be simple to one person could be extraordinarily difficult to achieve for another. In addition, the emotions related to the actual act of courage are equally important. The feelings of failure for not being courageous, as well as the euphoric sensation one gets when achieving success courageously are very much the same—from small, personal victories of courage, to life-saving acts of heroic courage.

Red Suit *(Six of Hearts)*

Intuiting this card in this position suggests you have successfully dealt with or faced a person or situation in your life that required some degree of courage. Courage has many hats, only one of which is to be heroic in the face of great peril. Each day, we all are required to be courageous in many ways. Defending a principle to an opposing person; changing a bad habit; confronting a situation or a person who is not being helpful or loving to you (for whatever reason); dealing with grief from the physical loss of a loved one; recovering from an illness; or coping with the ending of a relationship that was not meant to be. All of these and countless other scenarios require some degree of courage.

Recently you have been courageous either to yourself, to another, or for someone else which precipitated your selecting this card. Think deeply about your interactions with others and your personal deliberations about your life that required you to be courageous. Relish the fact that the Universe is recognizing you and your courageous deeds. Tread softly, but go courageously, dear fellow journeyer.

Black Suit *(Six of Clubs)*

Facing an area of our life that is unsavory takes great courage. Ignoring, abandoning or letting fester a situation that is causing you distress will only make it worse if you do not deal with it properly. Eventually, you will be forced to face the fear, danger, anger or pain. By waiting, you are expending negatively valuable energy that could be directed positively. All of these negative emotions usurp your personal power by stealing away your healing, loving energy. Bad energy craves good energy and will try to steal it anytime it gets a chance.

You intuited this Black Suit card because there is an area, an issue, or a person in your life that requires you to take a courageous stand. Spirit is encouraging you to center, focus, and conquer this issue which is causing you distress. No matter what it is, large or small, once you face it with your personal courage filled with light and love, you will release and conquer it. Be brave, be hopeful, be honest, and be courageous. In your heart, deep within your soul, you know the situation for which this card refers. Isn't it time to take care of it so you can get on with your journey? Your angels and guides are with you and will give you the strength you need.

Healing Intention

"I am courageous in my daily life. I conquer with courage, borne out of love, any false attitudes, misdirected beliefs, or unhelpful habits from this point forward. I wish for others the power to have the courage they need to continue on their journey. As I progress on my journey, I have the courage to confront anyone or anything that hinders me in a negative way. I offer this intention with love and healing."

Reflective Questions for your Self-Healing

-Why did I choose the card in the position I did?
-What lesson can be learned by focusing on this card?
-How do I interpret the meaning of this card?
-Why is this card significant to me at this moment?

Creativity

With loving thanks to our Creator, *creativity* is an ability or power that we all possess in wonderful abundance. It does, however, seem to come easier to some people than to others. If creativity isn't already a part of your everyday life, it can be. It doesn't have to be a concept that you only use to refer to others and their lives. It can be a viable part of yours.

Creativity can be a normal part of your life by simply allowing it to manifest from within. By consciously fostering your creative self, you tap into a vast personal reservoir that is uniquely your own; a natural resource—limitless and divine—a creative fountain, gushing and pouring forth lavishly.

Sadly, there are people who insist that they have no creative ability whatsoever, when in fact they are highly creative without realizing their special talent or knack which is a part of who and what they are. It is so crucial for a person's own spiritual well-being and further advancement on his/her life's journey to look within to find that special God-given talent that is bursting to come out. To do so is to become more of who you are meant to be. Open and allow your inner creative juices to flow like a river. Focus your loving, healing thoughts and energy on manifesting a creative life.

Red Suit *(Seven of Hearts)*

Choosing this Red Suit card is encouraging you to reflect upon your own abilities and strengths, and to go forward in creating something either tangible, like an object, or intangible, like an attitude or belief. Whether it is something that you can touch physically, or feel intuitively, it is still nonetheless creating. Creating and fostering creativity gives you the license and freedom to personally design the life that you want to live.

Two primary characterizations of this word are originality of thought or inventiveness. Being artistic or adept at "creating" things is only one part of this lovely word. You also have the power from within to create a life-purpose, a new attitude, an original idea or an item that is useful, beneficial and good for you. Don't limit your options by focusing on a narrow meaning or idea of this word. You have everything you need at your disposal. Go ahead and use your imagination…and create with abandon!

Black Suit *(Seven of Clubs)*

Recognizing and acknowledging the creative aspirations of others may allow you the opportunity to appreciate situations in your own life, which will in the long run help you to be more creative.

By selecting the card in this position, it is possible that you need to become aware of the creative happenings that are occurring around you. So much can be learned from observing and taking note of the creative aspirations of others.

Or, perhaps, you are not utilizing your full creative potential at present and are in need of focusing more clearly on this aspect of your life. Remember, creativity not only can refer to making or creating objects, but can also be related to abstract notions such as creating a new life, finding a new direction in which to go, or in developing a new attitude. A new spin on an old saying is: "A *creative* mind is a terrible thing to waste!"

Healing Intention

"I permit myself the freedom to create with abandon and to allow my creative juices to flow freely. My creativity will allow me to live happily and to think positively. I appreciate the creativeness in oth-

ers in order to be more creative myself. I offer this intention with love and healing."

Reflective Questions for your Self-Healing

-Why did I choose the card in the position I did?
-What lesson can be learned by focusing on this card?
-How do I interpret the meaning of this card?
-Why is this card significant to me at this moment?

Devotion

The earnest expression of profound and dedicated *devotion* is one of the most effective ways to connect easily and directly with the Divine. Spirituality, and the sincerity of the devotion associated with it, has more to do with what a person *does*, rather than what a person *believes*.

How people express devotion is very personal—the individual beliefs associated with a person's spirituality differ widely from one person to another. The daily ritual of showing devotion (no matter where or how it is done) and the intention behind the act of devotion, decides a person's level of true devotion. Belief systems vary, but the devotion to them stays constant.

The manner, in which people choose to conduct themselves in everyday situations, is related to the devotion they possess in their spiritual lives. Offering devotion consistently and frequently in our spiritual traditions allows us to connect with the Divine on a personal level, which is continuous and intimate. Also, by having devotion as a daily part of our lives helps us to center and ground our "spiritual-selves" with our "physical-selves."

As spiritual beings, we and only we have true control over our thoughts, actions, and beliefs. Only we can change our inner world to match the outer world we desire. By making devotion to God a priority, through a sincere reflection of our belief systems, can we effectively and accordingly change the outer world we experience. It is necessary to surrender completely to love and Spirit all our feelings of doubt, fear, anger, and hate. Then we can concentrate concretely on offering devotion to God that has purity of motive and sincerity of intention. We attract the type of people and situations we project (*e.g.* The Universal Law of Attraction—like attracts like).

Honoring Spirit by setting aside time on a daily basis to offer earnest devotion to our belief systems will clearly and consistently focus our intention to the Universe. In turn, the Universe will bestow all the wonderful riches of living a life of heartfelt devotion.

Red Suit *(Eight of Hearts)*

Living a life rich with *devotion*, whether it is to a belief system, a cause, or an ideal, has earned you accolades from the Universe. "Devotion" is most commonly associated with religious consecration, but it can also refer to a situation (*e.g.* a marriage, significant other, or work/family/ friend relationship); or a cause (*e.g.* dedicated service to an organization, volunteerism, a belief system).

The point is people have a variety of ways they demonstrate devotion, which is consistent and constant—some more religiously based than others. Most importantly, however, is proceeding with devotion that is from a pure heart and that is sincere in intention. This is all that is necessary to connect with the Divine that is within us all.

Having devotion in your life has enriched you greatly. Continue your devotion, and in the process, pause to thank the Creator for all the blessings and goodness that are bestowed upon you each and every day.

Black Suit *(Eight of Clubs)*

How do you personally define "devotion?" Is it being a good parent or partner? Son or daughter? Is it attending church on Sundays? How is devotion a part of your life? Is it a daily ritual or a sporadic event in times of great need?

You intuited this card because on some level, an aspect in your life or your idea of devotion is not completely without ulterior motive and not entirely borne from pure intentions. Faithfully assisting someone you love (a friend, spouse, partner or family member, or any number of possible scenarios) can only be regarded as devotion as long as it is not tainted with resentment or malice. Outwardly appearing to have devotion is different from actually possessing the aptitude and sincere desire to act it out.

For example, donating your money or your time to a worthy charity is a form of devotion…but only doing so because you can use it as a tax write-off cancels out the positive vibrations that would be generated if it were done without motive for self-gain. The best illustration, perhaps, related to the idea of "false devotion" is attending church on Sundays—not because you want to worship the Lord, but because you want to facilitate the appearance of being Godly to others who may see you there. Physically sitting in a pew does not make a person devoted—the act of going to church is meaningless if it is not accompanied by a pure heart and done with pure intentions. Many people wrongly equate going to church with being devoted. Many worshipers who attend church regularly are genuinely devoted to God, but so are many others who worship in their homes or other sacred places.

"Sunday only" worshipers may be attending church out of a need to impress, or to appear more virtuous in the eyes of other worshipers in attendance alongside them. This type of ulterior motive, laden with impure intentions only sullies the energy that is attributed to being that of "devotion."

Perhaps the Universe is gently reminding you to reassess honestly and sincerely your acts of devotion. Ask yourself, from the depths of your soul, the hard questions regarding how you define and perceive devotion. How can you purify or increase the devotion you desire to give? Follow instinctively the intuitive sensations and visions you receive when asking yourself these questions.

Offer the devotion God deserves with a pure heart and without motive—offer it unconditionally. If you follow your heart and intuition, you will be able to reflect positively, honestly, and sincerely upon the devotion you offer.

Healing Intention

"I consistently offer sincere devotion to our Creator which is pure and without ulterior motive. I strive and succeed to be a spiritual being who is deliberate in offering profound and dedicated devotion to God. I conduct my life on a daily basis that is rich in loving and blessed devotion in all that I do, say and feel. I offer this intention with love and healing."

Reflective Questions for your Self-Healing

-Why did I choose the card in the position I did?
-What lesson can be learned from focusing on this card?
-How do I interpret the meaning of this card?
-Why is this card significant to me at this moment?

Empower

Empower. This word evokes strength and authority. It is an enabling word, encouraging us to permit ourselves to be our best. Some people have the natural ability to empower themselves through positive thinking, a high self-esteem, or with an air of self-confidence. Others, unfortunately, forfeit their own empowerment by not following what they feel or want from the core of their soul, but by what others want or expect of them. This usurping of one's own empowering thoughts or heart-generated feelings by another has a draining affect on the person, in that it relinquishes the power of his/her all-encompassing life-force energy.

Empower yourself and empower others with the ability to pursue life with gusto. Following your life path honestly is a necessary process in understanding yourself more fully, and in progressing on your journey more completely. *Empower.* What a wonderful word!

Red Suit *(Nine of Hearts)*

The fact that you intuited this card suggests that you are well on the road to self-empowerment...or are already there! Spirit allows all of us the opportunity to have a feeling of empowerment, but not all of us choose to accept and utilize it.

In some way, you have. Perhaps recently you changed an old habit or way of behaving which has somehow empowered you. Or maybe, in a loving way, you empowered a fellow journeyer who was in need of some healing energy. Maybe by offering some encouraging words or by offering a supportive gesture or action you ultimately aided him/her. It is important to remember a cardinal rule of Spirit: "When you sin-

31

cerely help another, you are actually helping yourself." All occurrences which happen in the course of our life's journey, and the people we meet along the way, are related on some level—every action causes a reaction.

Concentrate deeply upon this healing word. The act or acts that precipitated your drawing this card may very well appear to you. If and when they do, be sure to make a mental note of what they are. Then you can go back and repeat them in kind to perpetuate more empowering good works, whether it is for you or for someone else. In the end, the one who benefits the most from these acts is you!

Black Suit *(Nine of Clubs)*

Empowering yourself is admirable, but doing so at the expense of others is not. You intuited this card because you are at odds with the issue of empowerment. Empowering yourself to be your best must come from a pure heart and with only the most honest of intentions—not from a selfish desire to tread upon others who are traveling on their journeys.

Words and actions toward another, which are made at their expense and not for their helpful benefit, may make you think you feel empowered, but this is short-term at best and is actually a false feeling. It is the same as when a child bullies another child on the playground; the feeling at that moment makes the bully feel empowered, but it is fleeting. The void, which precipitated the need to exert power over the weaker person, is still there...and will continue to be there until the void is filled with a sense of self-love, healing and compassion. This is true whether it involves a physical altercation, gossip, unkind thoughts, or pure spite. When you say or do something hurtful toward another, it is hurtful to you. Every thought, every word, every intention has a cause and effect relationship: all actions cause a reaction. You may be able to outwardly fool those around you, but you can't fool yourself. You know the intent behind the action and only you can remedy bad intentions by replacing them with pure, loving ones.

A feeling of superiority toward a fellow journeyer must not be confused with a feeling of genuine empowerment. Go into the wound to seek out why you intuited this card in this position. Search honestly and search deliberately. The answer awaits you. Find it. Face it. Conquer it. Release it.

The flip side of the "empowerment issue" coin may mean you are being denied a feeling of empowerment because of the people with whom you choose to associate. Don't forfeit your own empowerment to satisfy another's own needy, selfish agenda. Given the chance, and oftentimes without consciously realizing it, people steal another's life-force energy through control, manipulation, and guilt. In these cases, it is important to reverse these trends by taking control of *your* life by concentrating on your needs for empowering yourself through acts of love, compassion and healing.

Balance is the key, dear fellow traveler. You must focus on your own self-empowerment, which is done with a pure heart, and without treading on others to achieve it.

Healing Intention

"I empower myself lovingly and honestly. I feel the power of self-empowerment through my loving acts, thoughts, deeds, and intentions. I choose not to forfeit my own empowerment and I choose not to disempower another fellow journeyer through my actions or attitudes. I offer this intention with love and healing."

Reflective Questions for your Self-Healing

-Why did I choose the card in the position I did?
-What lesson can be learned by focusing on this card?
-How do I interpret the meaning of this card?
-Why is this card significant to me at this moment?

Enlightenment

On a soul level, all seek *enlightenment* as the ultimate reason for existence, and it is the primary reason why we all experience innumerable life cycles. The means, or process, to achieve this desired end-result is of most importance. Have you ever wondered what people mean when they refer to another person as being "enlightened?" Has this person already achieved their soul's desire and purpose?

No. But it does mean that the person who seems wise beyond his/her years is most likely living life in the positive and has figured out life's secrets by following his/her intuition, or "soul's desire." This type of person is progressing along the life-path (an integral part of the soul's journey), and has already experienced a variety of necessary life-episodes in this and past lives. Ultimately, this has made that person more aware and wise (primarily on a soul level, but also on the physical plane). The two go hand-in-hand. The physical, earthly experiences a person encounters affect the soul's spiritual journey. The knowledge from these experiences is then transferred in layers (*i.e.* lifetimes) to the soul's collective knowledge of these past experiences. This knowledge then influences the person on the physical, emotional, mental, and spiritual level of the next life cycle.

All the souls alongside you partaking, experiencing, and rejoicing in life are "souls in progress." Just like a "work in progress" sign on a highway, so are our souls as they proceed on their most wonderful journeys. The key is to avoid the major "detours" along the way whenever possible. These bypasses take us from the soul's intended path and slow down our progress. Each section of this spiritual highway has meaning and purpose…even the detours. All souls are meant to experience and learn from a variety of circumstances, situations, joys, and hardships as earthly beings in life cycles. These add to the soul's growth and wisdom.

All souls experience wealth, poverty, ill health, good health, being black, white, yellow and all the shades, shapes, sizes and orientations in between. As well, souls experience the celebrations and prejudices of being born into every ethnic and socio-economic background that there is. Ultimately, these collective experiences help to define what the soul is destined to do and to become. All the experiences of countless lifetimes overlap on a soul level. Consequently, what the soul is experiencing at this point in time, in this lifetime, on this planet called Earth, becomes valid and worthwhile.

Often, people refer to another person as having an "old soul." This refers to that person's current place in the Universe and that soul's collective *karma* which is all a part of the soul's spiritual journey. Each soul is at a different stage in the life-drama, having experienced lives and situations different from every other person. If some people seem to be further along on their life journey, and seem more enlightened, it is because they are. It is important to keep in mind that on some level, every soul is an "enlightened" soul insomuch that every soul has experienced, is experiencing, and will experience the necessary episodes of the life-drama which will aid it in reaching its ultimate soul purpose. Experience is the best teacher. Our all-loving God knows only too well how necessary it is for each soul to encounter all possible scenarios in its multiple lifetimes to reach a state of complete love, tolerance, acceptance and perfection, freeing it from all earth-bound suffering and physical desires.

Red Suit *(Ten of Hearts)*

Progress is being made on your soul's journey. Spirit is recognizing you for your steady advancement in the direction of achieving your soul's purpose. A truly enlightened person does not sit and gloat on the fact that s/he is in such a state—an enlightened person continues to strive forward by moving toward a more perfected form of enlightenment.

You are traveling resolutely in the direction you are supposed to be going. Continue your journey by following your intuition and by listening to your heart. The road to enlightenment is long, but be glad you are going in the right direction!

Black Suit *(Ten of Clubs)*

Being enlightened is a state of being. Sometimes people consider themselves to be very enlightened, but in fact are not because their "enlightenment" is not borne out of a sense of love and compassion, but one that is self-centered and self-serving. These people often are espousing attitudes and ideas that are misleading and perplexing. It is important not to negate categorically an ideology, doctrine, or philosophy just because it does not conform to your idea or opinion of what *you* believe to be true. "Truth" comes in many forms.

All the glorious people inhabiting our planet, hailing from a variety of different cultures and religious backgrounds, are moving toward the same goal of living a life which is rich in spiritual goodness and abundance. The only real differences are the rituals involved (the means of doing so and the systems used to worship God). It is important not to limit oneself by focusing upon a narrow interpretation of one particular belief system. This may impede one's ability to view others as equals. All are equal in the eyes of our Creator. Having a superior attitude towards others' beliefs is self-righteous and hypocritical.

A wondrous variety of beliefs, concepts, principles and ideals have been set before us to insure that we—all of God's children—are exposed to the assorted types of rationale the world has to offer. Following your beliefs fervently is noble; negating all other dogma or religions categorically with no real knowledge or understanding of them is irrational. Who are we to judge another of God's children?

A person on the right path to enlightenment maintains a respectful balance in his/her opinion of others' beliefs. This balance is nurtured and grown from a sense of tolerance and acceptance of what the other person believes (this is not to suggest that you should blindly accept all belief systems—many unhealthy and dark groups do exist and are put before us to test how well we can discern good from evil). A difference in ideology does not necessarily make a person or group "evil," but how magnanimously you accept others who are different does give a clue to how "enlightened" you truly are. It is necessary for you to decide prudently from within which tenets are harmful and which are not.

Accepting through tolerance and understanding another journeyer will help you to become more enlightened in this life cycle. Be cognizant of how you accept and reject people. Also, learn to discern honestly between those whom you reject from ignorance or a lack of knowledge and understanding, and those whom you choose not to associate with because they truly do threaten your continued progress on the path to enlightenment (in a harmful way). Always keep in mind that just as you may severely judge another because of his/her beliefs, so shall others judge you for yours. You receive back what you give. It is your choice to choose love and understanding over hate and intolerance.

Take a moment to reflect upon your own belief system, set of ideas, and personal opinions. How do these relate to your brothers and sisters who are traveling alongside you on their journeys? How can you be more tolerant and understanding? Ultimately, how can you become more accepting? The mere act of thinking about these questions will help to make you more enlightened.

Healing Intention

"I continue my journey of enlightenment by seeking answers to my questions with a pure heart and with the best of intentions. I offer hope and acceptance to all of my brothers and sisters who are seeking enlightenment with honest and pure hearts, that they too find the truths they are searching for, even if their methods and beliefs differ from those of mine. I offer this intention with love and healing."

<u>Reflective Questions for your Self-Healing</u>

-Why did I choose the card in the position I did?
-What lesson can be learned by focusing on this card?
-How do I interpret the meaning of this card?
-Why is this card significant to me at this moment?

Faith

People who have a strong spiritual *faith* by example often inspire faith and understanding in others. One's faith in his/her beliefs and principles is an admirable, even worthy virtue. However, forcefully imposing one's faith on others is not so appealing.

We all must proceed upon our own individual journeys in order to discover the answers to our particular life's questions. One can offer reflection to those who are searching for their life purpose best by demonstrating their own faith with purity of motive. We must respect and await another's decision not to pursue their spirituality until it is the right moment for them.

Trying to force a fellow person into Spirit will ultimately push the person away. Be patient, and be an example to others by living your faith purely and sincerely.

Red Suit *(Jack of Hearts)*

Selecting this card in the Red Suit suggests that you are traveling quite nicely and steadily on your journey. You are discovering your life purpose gradually, but sincerely, by conducting your life in a positive manner.

Spirit had you intuit this card in order to allow you some time to reflect on what you have accomplished up to this point in your life. Oftentimes we get so caught up in "life" that we don't stop to assess what we have successfully achieved. Also, this could be a little harbinger to let you know that by your example you are having a positive influence on one or more of your friends or colleagues. Keep the faith.

You *are* making a huge difference in this world and to those around you.

Black Suit *(Jack of Clubs)*

Life is full of ups and downs. At times we question our faith when obstacles are thrown into our life path (but are in actuality opportune reminders telling us to center, focus and proceed). Everything in life offers a learning experience. It is important to take the time to search for the reason behind the action or occurrence. This is not merely chance. There are no accidents.

Perhaps lately you have been feeling let down by someone or something in your life and in turn your faith has waned. Choosing this card is a gentle nudge to encourage you to concentrate more deeply on your beliefs and the reasons behind them. Blindly following an idea or belief without internalizing the reason and purpose behind it will leave you empty. Focus intently on this card and open yourself up to the healing energy it offers. Allow yourself to intuit what your guides are offering you. You will be amazed at what you'll see, hear, or feel.

Healing Intention

"I will follow my convictions and be true to my faith so that others may be inspired by my example. I embrace my faith with purity of motive and a sense of balance from within. I offer this intention with love and healing."

Reflective Questions for your Self-Healing

-Why did I choose the card in the position I did?
-What lesson can be learned by focusing on this card?
-How do I interpret the meaning of this card?
-Why is this card significant to me at this moment?

Forgiveness

Offering *forgiveness* to another is not an act you do for the benefit of someone else, as much as it is an act of self-healing you do for yourself. Too often when people offer forgiveness, conditions are placed on the "forgivee." More emphasis is erroneously placed by the "forgiver" on the need for the other person to admit they were wrong, than on the simple act itself.

The truth is that the person to whom you are offering forgiveness may or may not have the will or desire to accept, to recognize, or even to want your forgiveness. And that's OK. The act of offering forgiveness, made with sincere intentions and purity of motive, releases you from the negative energy associated with the act or deed that precipitated it. This simple act allows you to move past the person or action blocking your ability to let go of negatively generated feelings and emotions. It enables you to concentrate on more worthwhile endeavors by focusing on the positive aspects of your life and purpose.

As a spiritual journeyer, it is important to keep in perspective the reason why you are here in God's earthly garden—to experience, in a physical sense, the multitude of junctures which make up your current life. Your soul chose to participate in this life in order to further itself on its journey. Each situation experienced and each person encountered—good and bad—are a part of the whole. When combined together, all facets contribute positively to who you are as a person...and what you are to become. These life-experiences are all helping your soul to mature and to reach its divine purpose.

The need to forgive, and the actions which precipitated this need, are also necessary parts of your soul's maturation process. Offering forgiveness to others (and accepting forgiveness when it is given to you) releases you from the negative forces associated with it. The progress you make on this spiritual journey is in part dependent upon your ability to offer and accept forgiveness lovingly.

<u>Red Suit</u> *(Queen of Hearts)*

Offering forgiveness, which is filled with healing love and light, allows you to rise above negatively-generated energy, thus lifting the burden of being connected emotionally, mentally and spiritually to the situation or person which caused the bad feelings in the first place.

Bravo! The Universe recognizes your sincere efforts in the glorious realm of forgiveness. Does this intuited card refer to a situation where you forgave an unkind act done upon you…or did you accept forgiveness from a person who offered it to you for a past indiscretion…or could it refer to an act of forgiveness you offered lovingly to yourself? Too often, people find it easier to forgive others than themselves. It is as important to forgive yourself (if it is done with sincere atonement and with sincere intentions) as it is to find forgiveness in your heart for others.

Hold the Red Suit forgiveness card between your clasped hands and think deeply to whom or to what it may be referring. Enjoy the peace of mind that comes from putting the act of forgiveness into action; for taking control of your life and personal emotions. You cannot control anyone else's actions or intentions, but you certainly can control your own. By choosing to reclaim your sense of "self," you gain the needed confidence to forge on toward your life's purpose. Forgiveness allows you to deny consciously the entry of negative energy into your being and psyche.

Friend, relish the love, healing and light this compassionate act of forgiveness produced. When faced with a forgiveness decision in the future, always refer back to this feeling of profound release. It will help you to repeat the loving act of forgiveness when the occasion calls. Go, dear one, and continue to live your life with forgiveness.

Black Suit *(Queen of Clubs)*

"Forgive and forget." Seems simple, does it not? Unfortunately, it is not as easy as these three little words would like us to believe. Even when a person can find it in his/her heart to forgive, it is virtually impossible to forget the unkind act completely. Constant daily reminders of the unforgivable act can pervade your mind, life, and being. The act that precipitated the need for forgiveness in the first place is seemingly always there.

Perhaps a different approach is necessary to overcome the negative energy associated with the inability to completely "forgive and forget." It may be best to try and just "forgive," accepting the reality that you shan't ever really "forget." A time will come when it will not be as consuming as it is now, and the obsession that was related to it will gradually abate.

If you find yourself in this situation (where you are having difficulty in forgiving someone for an injustice done to you), focus all of your energy on the act of forgiveness. This is the most important part in the process of completely forgiving the person you feel has wronged you. Say aloud "I forgive you, not for your sake, but for my sake. I release you and the negatively-charged energy that currently bonds and connects us. I forgive you with pure intentions, and in the process I offer you love and healing."

In addition, it is cathartic to perform an actual purging ritual. You can do this by physically writing all of the yet-to-be-forgiven acts on a piece of toilet paper. Next, methodically and conscientiously, physically release them by flushing the paper down the toilet. While doing so, vigorously brush your arms with your hands (in a downward motion, from your shoulders to the tips of your fingers) getting rid of the negative energy associated with it. Attach the negative energy to what you forgave, and visualize them being flushed away, leaving you forever. Or write them in your hand by air-signing them into your palm. Then, blow them hard and visualize them floating out of the window far and away from you.

These acts of releasing the negative energy associated with what you need to forgive—whether it be anger, hate, disappointment, bitterness, guilt, or any of the other myriad of possibly negatively generated emotions—lifts your energy-level immediately. This allows you to pursue your life journey without the heavy burden from the refusal to forgive. The conscious decision to refuse forgiveness carries with it a connection, or earthly bond, that is enveloped in negative energy. This negative bond will follow you, wherever you go. If you do not take care of releasing it properly, it will even follow you into your next incarnation.

Now, let's focus on the *forgetting* portion of the formula to "forgive and forget." The best gift you can give to yourself is to forgive; the second best is to try and forget. If you cannot forget, then at least acknowledge the fact that you cannot forget the injustice done to you. By doing so you will release the negatively charged energy which is currently disallowing you from releasing the emotions connected to the act completely. Say aloud, "I acknowledge that I can forgive you, but I cannot forget what you did. By acknowledging the fact that I forgive you completely, I also acknowledge that I will not forget it. I do release the negative emotions and energy connected to what you did to me completely. In time, it will not matter that I remember except that it will remind me of where I have been and how far I have come. I offer this intention of acknowledgement with love and healing."

You intuited this card because you are at odds with an issue that concerns your willingness or ability to forgive completely. Remember, your forgiveness is not something you do for someone else; it is something that is necessary that you do for you. Follow the above prescription to release, once and for all, the resentment you are harboring for no good reason. It is certainly not good for you, and you are the one being hurt the most by it. Forgive, my friend, and in the process release.

Healing Intention

"I offer forgiveness, which is full of love and healing, to those whom I feel have wronged me. I offer forgiveness to myself for all the wrongs that I may have perpetrated on others or onto myself. I lovingly accept forgiveness from another who felt wronged by me when offered purely and lovingly. I hope that all will accept and offer forgiveness when the need arises. I offer this intention with love and healing."

Reflective Questions for your Self-Healing

-Why did I choose the card in the position I did?
-What lesson can be learned by focusing on this card?
-How do I interpret the meaning of this card?
-Why is this card significant to me at this moment?

Hope

People who have *hope* against all odds are truly the enlightened ones. Without hope, life would cease to exist as we know it. Offering hope to the seemingly hopeless is a gift that cannot be compared to any other.

Having hope for the future will ensure the survival of humankind. After all, a feeling of hope is so much more powerful and stronger than a feeling of despair. We have Spirit to thank for making this so.

Red Suit *(King of Hearts)*

Being hopeful and offering hope are virtues. This card suggests that you have done either one, or both, of these things recently. Allowing yourself to have and offer hope is like praying. The mere act of hoping in a positive, unselfish way is like sprinkling prayers over all who come into contact with you and your life-force energy. Keep on sprinkling your hopeful vibrations, it is working!

Continue to hope for the future—that all may have the ability to have hope for the world, each other, nature and all the creatures that share God's earthly garden. Focus your thoughts and energy on this word in order to build your personal power of hope, that this ability may come more effortlessly, abundantly, and selflessly.

Black Suit *(King of Clubs)*

Thoughts create energy, and energy follows thought. Putting a particular thought into the Universe is very serious business. It is necessary to only exude positive energy and thought in order for this to reflect back in kind to you. Negative thinking creates negative energy that in turn makes for unsavory experiences. Don't sabotage yourself by concentrating on the negative.

Perhaps recently you have lost hope in a situation, a person, or an idea. It is important for you to recognize the cause, and reverse this feeling of despair by focusing on the positive aspects of the situation. Never give up hope. It is always there and is yours for the asking.

Healing Intention

"I have hope for the world, its people, its plants and its animals—all of nature—that the future is a brighter, more peaceful one in which to live, heal and love. I offer this intention with love and healing."

Reflective Questions for your Self-Healing

-Why did I choose the card in the position I did?
-What lesson can be learned by focusing on this card?
-How do I interpret the meaning of this card?
-Why is this card significant to me at this moment?

Inspiration

At times, *inspiration* can appear like a meteor shower in the mind, flooding your being and essence with creative ideas and thoughts; other times we must seek out and then seize an inspired moment as if it were the last. Inspiration, like other states of mind and qualities of our existence, can be yours for the asking, anytime. Making a simple intention to the Universe to be inspired is all it takes.

The act of offering inspiration as an example to others can also aid your own inspired thoughts and feelings. Oftentimes we become so entangled in our own lives and projects that we sometimes forget to stop and take notice of others who may need an inspirational word to help them on their way. This conscious act of stopping to inspire another of God's children will in fact be beneficial to you in your journey. In addition, another person close to you may be able to offer a suggestion back to you which can aid you in your own creative, spiritual journey. Shhh…listen. You may be pleased with what you hear.

<u>Red Suit</u> *(Ace of Diamonds)*

The position of this card may mean that you are on the brink of realizing an inspirational idea or discovering from within yourself a concept which will aid you in your journey. While concentrating intently on the card, check the files of information you have stored in your mind. This will help you to focus in on the area of your life which precipitated your selection of this card.

Have you been mulling around an idea or notion but haven't felt the necessary inspiration to pursue it concretely or to act upon it? Now is your chance. Meditate upon this wonderful word, and an inspired thought on the relevant topic or situation will follow. A word of warning—have a pencil and some paper handy in order to jot down all of the wonderful insights that will saturate your mind's eye! Enjoy!

Black Suit *(Ace of Spades)*

Someone or something in your life, at work or at home, is in need of an inspiring word or action by you. Part of our purpose is not only to worry about our own, individual soul's journey, but to also aid our brothers and sisters in theirs when the need arises. Our journeys are not self-serving in that we concentrate solely on our own needs and desires. All of the people who are constantly guiding you, loving you, and serving you in your journey may need a helping hand in theirs. Part of our mission on this earthly plane is to offer assistance, love, and service to all.

Close your eyes and think deliberately about all those with whom you come into contact regularly. Try to remember anyone, in particular, who may have hinted about, outright asked you, or seemingly could have used a little inspiration. Perhaps Spirit is nudging you to guide or arouse the inspiration of another through Divine influence or intervention.

It is truly amazing the profound affect one person can have on another by simply offering a word of encouragement, a gentle act of kindness, or a genuine smile from the heart. Quietly focus on the card and most likely a person(s) or a situation(s) will appear to you which will answer why you intuited this card in the Black Suit. Go forth and inspire, dear friend!

Healing Intention

"I am inspired by my own essence and being. I will inspire and offer inspiration to others as often as I can. Those with whom I come into contact will inspire me with their comments, suggestions, and ideas

to aid me ultimately in my exciting journey. I offer this intention with love and healing."

<u>Reflective Questions for Self-Healing</u>

-Why did I choose the card in the position I did?
-What lesson can be learned by focusing on this card?
-How do I interpret the meaning of this card?
-Why is this card significant to me at this moment?

Joy

What is *joy*? Simply, it is anything that causes one to be happy. To feel joy, is to be happy. To be happy, is to feel love. To feel love, is to share with others. To share love, is to spread joy. Indeed, "joy" plays an integral role in producing a cycle of positive energy.

Having joy and being joyful is appreciating all that life has to offer in all its jubilant glory. Joy is the result of the many blessings afforded to you in the course of a day…a year…a lifetime. Joy is related to the feeling of gladness—both are compassionate and loving. Giving joy to another is an act of love that is pure and without ulterior motive. Receiving joy from another of God's children, if offered in love and accepted with appreciation, is a precious gift to be cherished.

Being joyful, having joy, giving joy and receiving joy—in any and all its stately and magnificent forms—is what makes living so important and worthwhile. Be joyful. Spread joy. And accept joy when it is offered to you. YES, joy is truly one of the simple pleasures that Spirit has so ingeniously afforded to us to savor in this earthly life.

Red Suit *(Two of Diamonds)*

God bless you! You have, gentle journeyer, recently experienced "joy" in some aspect of your life. Think deeply about all of the joy you are afforded in your life. What particularly stands out in your mind? Does it refer to being joyful? Having joy? Giving joy? Or did you receive joy from another? Perhaps it is a combination of all of these!

Experiencing joy in your life is so healthy for the mind, body, and spirit. It lifts the soul higher, allowing you to push forward on your journey, unimpeded, reaching and soaring ever upward. Like a kite floating in the wind, so does your soul get swept away in the healing energies that joy provides.

How wonderful that you are being recognized by Spirit and reminded by the Universe about how much, and in what ways, you have joy as a basic part of your daily life. It is due to people like yourself that there is hope and harmony for humanity, the world, and the Universe.

Scan your mind by closing your eyes; concentrate deeply on this energy enhancing word. Take a moment to thank God for all the joy you have. Count your joyful blessings by remembering consciously all the actions, situations, and people who have given or received joy as a result of you being you.

Black Suit *(Two of Spades)*

Some people close the door on joy, rejecting it at every turn. Why would someone want to deny him/herself this life-enhancing emotion? Often, it is not so much a conscious decision to live a joyless life, as much as it is one that has gradually occurred out of habit, guilt, or despair.

The old saying "misery loves company" conveys much truth. Sometimes people mistakenly believe that it is easier to stay in a wound, stoking the fires of distress, because it is familiar and seemingly safer. These people, either alone or with another with whom they feel a kindred connection, choose to seek solace and comfort from the negative energy generated in the wound...and from each other.

How misguided and debilitating this behavior and train of thought is to the person who is stuck in a rut that is void of joy. You intuited this card in the Black Suit because you are battling with a person, issue, or situation that is disallowing you from experiencing joy in its purest form. Some people are quite adroit at convincing another that it is better to stay in the wound rather than to acknowledge it and move forward, away from it.

Experiencing occasional sorrow is a necessary part of the trials and tribulations that accompany a human being's experiences here on earth. Each of us, on a soul level, chose our karmic destiny before incarnating into our current lives. The harder and more difficult the life-drama, the more refined the spirit and further we advance on our soul's journey.

People sometimes get caught in a vortex of negativity due to an unhealthy situation or relationship; having feelings of guilt or shame; or from experiencing deep sorrow (*e.g.* suffering the loss of someone they loved deeply and completely). Staying in a state of deep sorrow robs you of your life-enhancing energy, and hinders you from experiencing any real joy. Also, holding on to sorrow, by grieving profoundly over the death of a loved one for an extended period of time, will not assist the person in transitioning easily into Spirit. It is necessary for you to break the earthly bond that is formed through profound grief, in order to allow your loved one to pass over to the other side unimpeded.

Losing a loved one is devastating on every level, except one: The level in which the person had fulfilled his/her life purpose and mission for this incarnation. Be encouraged to know that the person you loved so dearly passed into Spirit having done all that his/her soul had intended him/her to do in this life. Be assured to know that the actual "death" set into motion a series of effects that will reverberate for an eternity. Just like a stone thrown into a pond, the waves scatter out evenly, affecting in some way everything in their path. The loved one's spirit is like a stone thrown into the sea of the Universe, affecting all whom s/he touched, reverberating for an eternity everything and all in his/her path. If you are lacking joy due to the loss of a loved one, and are wallowing in a sea of deep sorrow, you will drown if you don't pull yourself above the surface.

If familiarity of a person or situation is hindering you from breaking out of a negative cycle, then muster the strength and courage to reverse this destructive trend. Familiarity often breeds contempt; recognize it as such and remove yourself from it. It will take much courage to face the person and/or situation head-on. This is something you must do for yourself—not the other person. Only you have the ability to reclaim your life and to decide consciously to put joy back into your life.

Guilt and shame are emotions that can consume a person's energy at a dizzying pace. Like an avalanche storming down a mountain, the faster it goes the stronger it gets and the more momentum it has. Directly confront the guilt or shame you are feeling with honesty and healing love. You must get past this guilt or shame in order to continue on your journey. This may require you to forgive yourself. If this be the case, then do it. Forgiving yourself just may be the greatest gift you'll ever receive.

Living life in a cloud of joyless despair is unnecessary. What is necessary, however, is for you to reverse your attitude and feelings to recapture the lost joy.

Healing Intention

"I invite joy to enter my life and to pervade my being and essence in every way. I offer joy to others whom I meet. When offered joy from another, I accept it willingly for it is given lovingly. I harness and enjoy all the joy the Universe has to offer me. I offer this intention with love and healing."

Reflective Questions for your Self-Healing

-Why did I choose the card in the position I did?
-What lesson can be learned from focusing on this card?
-How do I interpret the meaning of this card?
-Why is this card significant to me at this moment?

Knowledge

Knowledge is power. Having knowledge about the world, Spirit, life, and ourselves gives us strength and power to conquer all obstacles that are placed before us in our personal lives and on our spiritual journey. Most misunderstandings people experience come from a lack of adequate knowledge about the situations to which they refer.

Ignorance is a symptom of having a lack of knowledge. Some people often quickly negate a religious tradition or belief, or reject a person because of his/her appearance, cultural background, or orientation—because of a lack of knowledge. Those who make snap judgments about a person based on such superficial criteria, without proper knowledge, are in fact doing themselves a great disservice. Much can be learned from the serendipitous opportunities God presents us with on our spiritual paths. Interacting with the wonderfully diverse range of people God allows us to meet while traveling sincerely along our life and soul journeys assists us on a soul level.

Being knowledgeable is taking control of your life and your actions. Gaining knowledge is an endeavor that will continue throughout your entire lifetime. Never pass up an opportunity to gain knowledge from others who are more experienced and wiser about love, life, Spirit, and the world. And definitely never pass up a chance to gain a deeper knowledge about yourself. It will help you to learn, understand, and accept all that is presented to you on this most wonderful soul journey.

<u>Red Suit</u> *(Three of Diamonds)*

Bravo, dear journeyer! The universe is giving you a well deserved pat on the back for seeking out and gaining some type of knowledge—whether it is about yourself, a loved one, a spiritual truth, or about love, life or Spirit in general. You are being acknowledged for your recent efforts in expanding your point of reference—seeking out answers to your questions—and for gaining knowledge in some area of your life.

Being knowledgeable is not the same as being a "know-it-all." It *is* being aware and open to what the world and God has to offer. When an opportunity presents itself to you to enhance your own personal knowledge about a particular subject, tradition, ideal or belief, it is nice to know that you (on some level) have embraced it with enthusiasm and a positive attitude.

Some knowledge that is gained in the course of our daily lives may be quite painful, especially that which makes us reevaluate ourselves in a critical, but honest way. But even in these instances, the knowledge gained empowers us to be stronger and clearer in our own personal life and in our beliefs.

Asking yourself "What knowledge can be gained from this occurrence?" has allowed you to harness a very important energy—the energy of self-empowerment—because knowledge is power. Continue your lifelong quest for knowledge. Godspeed, dear seeker of knowledge.

Black Suit *(Three of Spades)*

God is notorious for placing us in situations or with people who serve to test our sensitivities. These occurrences are not mere happenstance that can be shrugged off as coincidence or unimportant. They are valuable opportunities, which if pursued fully, will help us to grow personally, spiritually, emotionally, and mentally.

Knowledge can also be a learning experience learned from a bad situation or person who has caused you pain. The point of comparison between knowing definitely what it is you *don't* want (either in a personal, familial, or working relationship) is knowledge. Try not to discount automatically the negative occurrences in your life without first evaluating them for what they are—learning experiences that offer you more in-depth knowledge about yourself, others, and the world. These are valuable lessons that can teach you much about yourself and others if you approach them with an attitude of wanting to gain knowledge from them.

Perhaps recently you passed up a unique opportunity to further your knowledge about something or someone by allowing your own ego to disregard it without really investigating it thoroughly. Or maybe you had an opportunity to impart some of your knowledge to another of God's children but refused to do so for selfish reasons.

Knowledge teaches us discernment, and discernment is the hallmark of being a spiritual being. Without discernment, we cannot know what to accept and what to reject. Knowledge, dear journeyer, gives us the necessary tools to discern properly.

Rethink your recent interactions in a concentrated, methodical way. Did God place you in a situation, or with a person, which tested your knowledge in an intellectual, spiritual, emotional, or mental way? Were you given an opportunity to gain valuable knowledge about something, but chose not to pursue it? Be open to new things, ideas, and people who are different; be careful not to negate or reject out of hand that which could make you a more knowledgeable person. All is in Divine Order...but it is up to you to make it happen through life experience. Using your own ability to discern properly will aid you in gaining more knowledge.

Healing Intention

"I choose to empower myself with knowledge. I seek out and seize opportunities the Universe presents to me to gain more knowledge; this leads to understanding, which in turn allows me to discern for myself all that is and shall be. When appropriate, I offer my knowledge to others whom I meet while on my journey, which is full of love and light. I also accept knowledge from those who have knowl-

edge to offer me, and from situations in which I can gain discerning knowledge. I offer this intention with love and healing."

<u>Reflective Questions for your Self-Healing</u>

-Why did I choose the card in the position I did?
-What lesson can be learned by focusing on this card?
-How do I interpret the meaning of this card?
-Why is this card significant to me at this moment?

Love

Love is not only a beautiful word; it is also the greatest gift we can give to others…and to ourselves. In order to be loved, one must love oneself and others, unconditionally. So often we scurry about in search of love, or try to find the perfect love, that we don't stop to give love to ourselves or to offer loving thoughts and actions to those we come into contact with each day.

It is vitally important to take the time to recognize true love which is pure and without pretense; equally important is to learn to negate the aspects of what you think is a loving relationship, but in actuality only causes you distress, worry, and fear. These three negative feelings which are sometimes mistaken as necessary parts of love are not really related to love at all in its most basic and purest form. Love is not controlling. Love is not possessive. Love is not distressing.

Love is understanding. Love is accepting. Love is blissful. Love is kind. Love is pure. Always distinguish between "true" love and love borne out of false pretenses, jealousy and the need to control and possess. As the old saying goes, "If you love something, set it free…" In the process, you set yourself free.

<u>Red Suit</u> *(Four of Diamonds)*

How wonderful! You have intuited this card in recognition of your recent loving deeds, loving ideas, or pure love towards a partner or a mate. Perhaps you have a strong filial love for a child in your life. If none of these areas seem to apply to your current situation, then look within for the answer as to why you chose this card in this position.

Love has many hats, only one of which refers to the physical love we offer to a partner. Love is a versatile emotion and energy-generating word. It can refer to a loving attitude, a loving act, or an idea borne out of pure love. It can be a love that is compassionate, or a love that is sympathetic, helpful or assisting to another of God's precious children. Continue to love unconditionally. Recognize the love within yourself and the love you receive from others with whom you come into contact on a daily basis.

<u>Black Suit</u> *(Four of Spades)*

Love is a powerful emotion, which when used positively can be exhilarating. But love borne out of jealousy will drain a person dry of his/her life-giving energy. Wasting vital life-energy on negative aspects which involve obsessive love, unrequited love, a controlling love, a spurned love, or a jealous love will not help you spiritually to further yourself on your life path.

Reflect honestly upon all of your relationships—from your partner all the way to the stranger on the street. With a spouse or partner, are you offering a love that is jealous? As a parent, are you trying to control in the name of love a situation that is not yours to control? As a lover, are you being possessive and demanding in your love? As a child, are you manipulating the loving emotions of a parent or guardian? As a co-worker or a boss, are you being unloving and insensitive to the needs of those around you? As a friend, does your love promote your own agenda that may be for selfish-motives? As a stranger on the street, do you offer love in the form of tolerance, courtesy, and goodwill to those whom you meet?

You intuited this card in the Black Suit indicating you need to review your relationships of the heart. Look deep from within and go directly into the wound to pull out any potentially negative aspects of this otherwise beautiful, positive, and exhilarating emotion. Release any negative vibrations you have been harboring in the name of love. By doing so, you will release the dark cloud hanging over you which is currently absorbing your beautiful, God-given energy. Replace this void with clear, warm, bright, positive, and loving energy.

Healing Intention

"I offer love to myself, unconditionally. I offer love to those whom are important to me in my life. I offer love to all whom I meet. I love without pretense, ulterior motives, or misguided desires in my daily life. My love is pure and it comes from the heart. I offer this intention with love and healing."

Reflective Questions for your Self-Healing

-Why did I choose the card in the position I did?
-What lesson can be learned by focusing on this card?
-How do I interpret the meaning of this card?
-Why is this card significant to me at this moment?

Peace

Being at *peace* with oneself is not only a significant personal victory; it is one of life's great achievements. Sadly, there are many people who live their entire lives without ever feeling true peace of mind. Why is this? Unfortunately, negative feelings and attitudes like guilt, anger, fear and disappointment invade the psyche of these people, disallowing them from having a sense of peace in their lives which is tranquil, serene, and loving.

Offering to make the peace with another journeyer with whom one is at odds will help both of you to release any of the aforementioned negative emotions. There is no practical reason to live life in a fog of guilt, anger, fear or disappointment when one can choose not to do so. In many instances, forgiving a person or yourself for a past indiscretion is all that it takes to find peace of mind. Other times, the act of offering forgiveness, as a way to make amends to another, is the best way to rise above the negativity that is perpetually generated by staying in the wound.

Finding forgiveness in your heart is not an act you do for someone else. It is something that you do for *you*. In fact, if it is indeed another who has trodden unkindly upon you, s/he may not know, accept, or feel that they have slighted you in any way. Your forgiveness is not so dependent upon their knowledge of your forgiveness as much as it is for you to know *you* have forgiven *them*, and with it released all the negativity attached to it. Once forgiveness is offered from the heart, the negative energy surrounding the person or situation is lifted and is released. A sense of peace can then fill the void left by the negative feelings that had been hindering your ability to find peace of mind.

Red Suit *(Five of Diamonds)*

Dear journeyer, your recent efforts in or success at making peace with another (...or with yourself) about an issue or situation which had caused you distress is recognized and duly noted by the Universe.

Finding this sense of peace from a personal perspective regarding an attitude, belief, or action that relates to your interactions with another, or a change you made within yourself is noble. Being at peace with another and having peace of mind allows you the freedom to develop a relationship with yourself, the other person, and with the Divine, which is compassionate and pure.

Consciously choosing to be in a state of harmony, free from strife and turmoil, allows you to enjoy and relish a feeling of serene tranquility. As a bonus, it also frees up necessary energy that is needed to pursue more relevant, loving, and healing endeavors.

You intuited this card in the Red Suit because of a recent occurrence involving effort on your part to choose peace over strife; to pursue actively peace of mind rather than turmoil. Regardless of whether the instance refers to the making of peace with another—or to you—at home, at work or at play, continue to pursue a peaceful existence. These loving vibrations and healing intentions envelop you and encourage those with whom you are associated and come into contact. Bless you, dear journeyer, bless you. Peace be with you.

Black Suit *(Five of Spades)*

It is important to make amends with people whom you find yourself at odds. "Making the peace" is very important in order to release your soul from any earthly bonds that are holding you in a pattern that is not allowing you to sow the seeds of progressive and positive change. Reliving the same issue time after time has you in a negative karmic cycle. Any unresolved issues you take into Spirit during this life's transitional death will follow you into your next incarnation. The people may look different, the situations may be different, but the unresolved issues and problems will still be the same, involving the same soul entities.

Finding peace of mind is equally important. When a person is living life in the positive, naturally a sense of peace follows—taking care of old business is the best place to begin to find peace of mind. Journeyers, who find themselves in situations where they have no peace of mind, or constantly are embroiled in strife, are disallowing the soul to move further on this life's journey. Those who live in the past are truly doomed to repeat it.

As a gift to yourself, it is necessary to release any anger or hurt you are harboring towards yourself or another, because it is hindering you from moving forward. Forgiving in a loving way, either yourself or another, will allow you to find the peace within yourself, which is what your soul so desperately desires. Being at peace with yourself and with others will allow you to soar higher than you ever thought possible.

You intuited this card in the Black Suit because you have a person or situation in your life that needs to be addressed fully, and then released in order for you to have peace of mind, be at peace with yourself, or to make the peace with another. If it involves offering an olive branch to another journeyer, take the initiative and make the effort to remedy the situation. Do you really want to carry this strife with you into your next life cycle?

However, dear journeyer, simply offering a goodwill gesture to make the peace, even if from a pure heart, does not necessarily mean the other person will accept it. Fortunately, the mere act of initiating the process, which is full of love, promotes at some level a healing, which in turn offers understanding. It will help you to clear the blockage that is holding *you* back. The various reasons the other person has for denying your loving gesture to make the peace (and the ultimate outcome of your loving action) is for that person to deal with personally and spiritually. The most you can do is to clear your conscience by making a concerted effort, which is sincere, from the heart, pure in intent, and full of love.

Concentrate deeply on the issue or person that is not allowing you to enjoy peace of mind; to be at peace with yourself or with another; or to initiate the process to make the peace. The situation, as well as peaceful solutions, will come forth from within.

Healing Intention

"I am at peace with the Universe. From within and for me, I have serene peace of mind. I offer peace to all whom I encounter. I offer this intention with love and healing."

Reflective Questions for your Self-Healing

-Why did I choose the card in the position I did?
-What lesson can be learned by focusing on this card?
-How do I interpret the meaning of this card?
-Why is this card significant to me at this moment?

Prayer

Prayer is a powerful tool. It allows us to have dialogue directly and personally with our Creator. Offering a prayer, which is earnest, reverent and pure is the most effective way to commune with God.

Why do we pray? Some people use prayer as a way to clear their minds of all the daily life-stuff, cleansing their being of negative thoughts and energy. Other people pray only in times of great need, while others make prayer a daily part of their lives. Some pray to express their hopes and desires. The majority of God's children, however, use prayer as a way to demonstrate their devotion to God—the divine power that is a part of each and every one of us.

Having some sort of prayer in your daily life-ritual will help you to define more clearly your aspirations, hopes, and desires, as well as to give you an opportunity to show Spirit the appreciation you have for all that you are afforded in this life. It will also help you to focus, in times of trouble, on issues and problems that need clarification and attention. Heartfelt, concentrated prayer (that is pure and full of love and light) gives you the most powerful tool you need to succeed in your life, and to overcome the occasional life-obstacles put before you.

Red Suit *(Six of Diamonds)*

Hallelujah! Praise the Lord! Glory be to God! Hosanna! Just thinking about these "prayerful" phrases energizes the soul. Imagine what they would do if you were to shout them out into the Universe! Prayer is an integral part of our spiritual life. It calms us physically and emotionally; it uplifts us spiritually and mentally; it allows us to focus clearly on issues and situations that affect our lives and our spiritual journeys.

You intuited this card in the Red Suit because you are aware (or on the brink of becoming aware) of the importance prayer has in your daily life—on a physical and soul level. "Prayer" can come in many forms other than that which is associated with the popular image of a child kneeling beside a bed, with hands in the traditional prayer position. A prayer can be offered anywhere and at anytime. This, however, is not to suggest that a prayer given on the "run," while doing three or four things at once, is as effective as one which is given from the heart, at a time that is especially set aside for prayerful devotion.

God isn't picky about where or when a prayer is offered. The important aspect of praying has to do more with the intention behind the prayer, rather than the time and place. Some people pray in the morning, evening...or both. Some people pray while meditating or walking through a forest. Others have a particular place of solitude where they can pray without distraction or interruption, while some choose to pray in locations that have a lot of activity going on around them, like at work or at home. But remember, when a prayer is offered, it should be at a time that allows full and undivided concentration—a specific time set aside in the day which is devoted solely to the act of praying; in a place that is comfortable and agreeable to you, both physically and spiritually.

Dear prayerful journeyer, continue using prayer in your daily life as a tool to allow you to see more clearly the divine connection which exists between you and God. Allow the abundance of the Universe to afford you what you need through prayer; show appreciation for all that Spirit has given to you by praying earnestly. Prayer...it is indeed a powerful, powerful tool.

Black Suit *(Six of Spades)*

Sometimes our spiritual journeys include life-obstacles, which on a soul level, are needed, appreciated, and relished. As earthly beings however, these "lessons" are, at times, hard to accept and understand for what they are. These experiences, in the whole scheme of one's entire existence in multiple lifetimes, are needed to help us proceed positively forward in achieving our soul's divine purpose.

Once an obstacle is thrown into our path—whether it be a person with whom we are at odds; a situation which causes us strife; an illness of the mind or body that needs healing; a broken heart from a love that didn't work out as we had hoped; or the death of a loved one with whom we had a strong, earthly bond—it is important to maintain balance in assessing the issue from a spiritual vantage point. It's at the times when we are at our lowest that make it all the more necessary to focus and proceed positively toward overcoming the stumbling block placed before us.

Prayer is the best way to take a life-challenge, which is seemingly negative or debilitating, and turn it into a positive, powerful life-force. Everything that occurs to us does so for a reason. Each person who crosses our life-path does so for a reason. It is important to keep in mind that all problems we face in life have a solution. Every action we incur has a reaction somewhere in the Universe. Praying to find the reasons behind occurrences and solutions to problems will help you in your spiritual quest to understand and to accept what happened.

As hard as it may seem to do, it is always helpful to sit and reflect inwardly during times of confusion and distress. This will help you to put the situation into better perspective. Also, it will allow you to connect the threads of your life's fabric to give you needed clarity in comprehending what happened and how or why it affects you in the way(s) it did. Ask yourself: how does what happened affect the other person(s) involved or the overall situation? How has this experience made me a stronger person? What have I learned from this experience?

Instead of thinking that things happen *to* you, maybe it is healthier to consider life's challenges as things happening *for* you. After all, much insight can be gained from adverse occurrences which affect you spiritually, emotionally, mentally, and physically. Try to focus on the intended "lesson" which is contained in these occasional trials, rather than concentrating on the negative aspects. It is more common for our ego to rationalize situations from a victim's standpoint and attitude, rather than from that of a survivor's. Reclaim the situation by reversing the negative spin put upon it. This will put the power and energy surrounding it back into your hands, making it yours once again.

Perhaps you selected this card in the Black Suit because you are at odds with how to proceed regarding a life-issue or circumstance; or you have lately neglected your spiritual needs by not taking the necessary time to pray. Oftentimes, when our lives become harried with duties and obligations, dealing with family, work, relationships and a myriad of other incidental life-related issues, we either consciously or unconsciously "triage" our daily responsibilities to accommodate all that we think has to be done. In the process, we sometimes tend to thrust aside more personal needs (like prayer, pampering, relaxation, meditation, etc), which require tending to just as urgently as other, more tangible life-related duties and obligations.

Take the necessary time to make prayer a meaningful and consistent part of your life. If you don't include prayer on a daily basis, start now! If you do pray regularly, but do not do so with a clear mind or at a designated time that is devoted solely to prayer, do so as soon as possible. Making prayer an integral part of your life will give you the necessary strength to tackle the occasional roadblocks you receive while continuing on your soul's journey.

Healing Intention

"I offer this prayer to our Creator lovingly, with a pure heart and earnest devotion. I pray for the well-being of the earth, its people and nature. I pray that I will follow my spiritual journey sincerely and earnestly. I appreciate all that is afforded to me in this life and I pray for the wisdom to recognize all of my blessings. I offer this prayerful intention with love and healing."

<u>Reflective Questions for your Self-Healing</u>

-Why did I choose the card in the position I did?
-What lesson can be learned from focusing on this card?
-How do I interpret the meaning of this card?
-Why is this card significant to me at this moment?

Promise

Making a *promise,* either to yourself or to others, is very serious business. Anyone who has had the unpleasant experience of having a promise broken will attest to this. It is not a good feeling, to say the least. A "cross your heart" type of promise is one, which should be made with only the highest level of integrity, and with the sincerest of intentions to carry it through to the end; it should also be made with an abundantly sprinkled feeling of hope for a positive and beneficial outcome.

Another meaning of this insightful word is to show or have promise, meaning "potential." We all have promise to be the best that we can be. Sometimes we need a little encouragement to help this "promise" surface and to come along. Offering "promise" to someone else is yet another take on this versatile word. To give promise to someone is to acknowledge his or her potential to succeed.

It is a truly special gift to make a promise to another or to yourself (and to keep it); to show promise by demonstrating your skills and abilities to others; to have promise by allowing your true potential to succeed; and ultimately to give to a person who is in need of hearing that s/he, too, has promise and potential to be the best possible person s/he can be. Promise, in all its various forms and meanings, is a truly special and loving word.

<u>Red Suit</u> *(Seven of Diamonds)*

"Promises, promises, promises" is a sarcastic lamentation by so many, so often, because promises are not always kept. It is no wonder people have become cynical of other people, or skeptical of organizations, which make promises. Keeping a "promise" that one makes to another person or to oneself should not to be taken lightly.

You intuited this card in part because you know the importance of keeping a promise; in offering promise to another; or by showing promise in yourself or to others. You are perhaps at the brink of letting shine a particularly promising career, attitude, idea or way of life, which will appear to you more clearly by concentrating on this word intently. Focus your energy directly to allow your promising characteristics, personality traits, or deeds to appear to you.

Black Suit *(Seven of Spades)*

Lately, perhaps you have felt discouraged because you feel you lack "promise" in a particular area, field or relationship. Maybe you made a promise but failed to keep it—whether it was to yourself or to someone else.

Perhaps you selected this word in the reverse position in order to reflect upon the situations in your life where you have "promise" but are not rising to your full potential. Maybe you have not shown adequate promise, even though it is indeed there within you (but is only in need of being developed). On the other hand, perhaps you knowingly made a promise that you knew you could not keep.

The reason that precipitated your intuiting this card is in your heart. You need to rectify the situation, whether it is to yourself or to another, by looking deeply at the attitude that is preventing you from achieving your full promise; or the failure to give promise to someone whom you know could use your heartfelt encouragement. Once you face this situation in your life, head on, you will feel much better. I promise!

Healing Intention

"I promise to fulfill my promises to others and to myself. I allow the promise I have within to show and shine in order to further me on my journey. I offer promise to others who need this encouragement

in order to help them along their journeys. I offer this intention with love and healing."

Reflective Questions for your Self-Healing

-Why did I choose the card in the position I did?
-What lesson can be learned by focusing on this card?
-How do I interpret the meaning of this card?
-Why is this card significant to me at this moment?

Respect

Respect is something that we all wish (or even demand) to have but it is something that we don't always offer or give to others or at times truly deserve for ourselves because of our actions or treatment of others. Why is that?

Part of the reason is that we get so caught up in our own lives, work, and family—putting ourselves at the center of our universe—that we fail to realize that we are each a reflection of everything else in the universe. If we fail to respect others, how can we expect to be respected?

Respect isn't only something we need for our egos and to nurture others' egos—it is necessary for our survival as an individual and as a member of the global village. Respect, and the deep understanding needed to fully comprehend it, is a part of our attitude toward not only people but to all aspects of life and Spirit.

Those who do not respect themselves or others likely do not respect Mother Earth and her life-giving gifts to humankind. People who do not offer respect to nature cannot understand fully all the beauty in everything that is available to us in this great big beautiful world. Having respect for life—including plants, animals, and fellow humans—fosters a healing attitude to living a life which includes a great element of love, compassion, and reverence for all that is around us and is a part of us.

Respect is something you earn. Respect is received by giving it to others. Offering respect that is pure and sincere to all forms of life will place you in a position of being the recipient of respect. Above all, be respectful to yourself by stopping to contemplate the glory that respect holds in your life…and in the lives of others.

Red Suit *(Eight of Diamonds)*

You intuited this card in the Red Suit because the Universe is commending you on your ability to respect and to have respect for either yourself, others, things, or all that is a part of your universe and the world. Respecting others, no doubt, has taught you a fundamental Universal Law—like attracts like. By offering and giving respect, respect comes back to you in a wonderfully positive cycle of loving energy.

Continue to take time to respect all that is available to you in God's earthly garden…especially, continue respecting yourself.

Black Suit *(Eight of Spades)*

It is all too easy for us humans to get so caught up in our own egos that we begin to drown in our own self-pity, barely able to keep our head above the bitterness and anger we sometimes feel toward others because of their actions toward us. We lament the saying "I get no respect."

If this is the case with you, stop to ask yourself why this is; what can *you* do to change this situation? Go deep inside and reflect honestly about respect and how you invoke the concept of respect into your life on a daily, consistent basis.

Often is the case where we tend to see the world through blinders—looking straight ahead at issues and problems that affect us directly, but failing to look at the peripheral sides of the situation. Acting respectfully toward everything and everybody will help others to see you in a light that merits newfound respect.

Or…perhaps you don't offer yourself a sufficient level of respect, which in turn is sending the wrong message out to others with whom you must deal and relate to. How can you expect others to respect you in the way you want them to, if you can't find it in you to offer yourself the amount of respect you truly deserve? The clearer the action is, the clearer the response by others is.

Look deep inside yourself to ask the hard questions of why you intuited this card at this moment. What message is the Universe trying to send to you? What can you do to aid being respected by others? How can you better respect others? Pray on it. The answers are within your reach. Grab them and hold them in your heart. Do what you have to in order to regain respect and to make respect a consistent part of your interaction with others in your daily life.

Healing Intention

"I respect myself, I respect others, I respect all living and non-living things in this wonderful world. I offer respect to myself, to others, and to all living and non-living things, so I may better reap the pleasure of having respect offered back to me reciprocally. I offer this intention with love and healing."

Reflective Questions for your Self-Healing

-Why did I choose the card in the position I did?
-What lesson can be learned by focusing on this card?
-How do I interpret the meaning of this card?
-Why is this card significant to me at this moment?

Tolerance

Tolerance can be defined as having the capacity to endure something physical, emotional, or mentally painful and hard. Fortunately for us, we can choose not just to "tolerate" unpleasant situations, attitudes or conditions we find ourselves in, but make the personal decision not to allow negative forces to dominate our being. We have the ability to negate such unsavory situations by simply choosing consciously to do so.

Indefinitely tolerating people and their actions, situations and conditions, which are negative in nature, is not helping you in the long run, and is certainly not beneficial to you or anyone continuing on his/her life's journey. Enabling a loved one by giving "unconditional tolerance" towards behavior or actions which are not healthy and positive is not the best path to follow. Distinguish the difference between your lovingly tolerating a situation or person, which is not beneficial to you and the possibility that your tolerance is selfish in nature, in order to avoid facing the truth. The unhealthy enabling of a person or situation under the guise of "loving tolerance" may be trapping you in a rut. If so, this negative cycle will constantly sap your energy in the process, which is damaging to both parties. One exception, however, is if you choose to recognize such "tolerance" as being unhealthy, face it head-on, and then release it and its negative vibrations completely. This will help you move forward.

There is a huge difference between "tolerating" and being "tolerant." It is important to be tolerant of others who may have beliefs and opinions that do not directly coincide with yours; but equally necessary is the importance to avoid the situation where you find yourself tolerating others who are only negative and vindictive towards you. In these cases, for your own spiritual peace of mind, it is necessary for you to choose not to tolerate certain people, situations, or conditions that only serve to distress you. You can do this by physically removing yourself from their presence or the situation; if this is not a possible option, then perhaps a viable solution would be to mentally distance yourself by concentrating on the positive energy.

Too much energy is wasted in tolerating people or situations, which become a test of endurance. In the end, it may not be helping you on your own life's path. You don't have to be a martyr to be compassionate and understanding. Possessing a loving tolerance of others, however, will allow your own compassionate spirit to serve as a beacon to those whose paths need light from your example of a tolerant and compassionate heart.

Red Suit *(Nine of Diamonds)*

Always doing the right thing is something that everyone would like to do on a consistent basis. It is so easy to judge another without thought to the conditions and situations that brought that person to the place where your paths crossed.

It is pleasing to know that you intuited this card in the Red Suit position, in part because you have shown tolerance towards another of God's children. Perhaps you have tolerated a hardship or painful situation, knowing intuitively from the depths of your loving heart that the nucleus of the act, person, or situation was necessary in the total process that allowed you to arrive where you are today. Offering a tolerant attitude to another person or situation has helped you to understand yourself more clearly and to accept yourself more fully.

Sometimes the opinions, beliefs and even actions of others are difficult to understand or to accept. By being tolerant, in a loving and healing way, you have offered a gift of love not only to the other person or situation, but also to yourself. The self-righteous judging of others and situations is one of life's many tests, which most of us mere mortals fail at miserably...and consistently. Perhaps recently you found yourself in a situation, which gave you a choice: 1) to be a tolerant, understanding, and accepting human being; or 2) a judging, intolerant creature. You chose the proper course to follow. Look within your heart and search for the situation to which this card refers…then rejoice. You deserve it!

Black Suit *(Nine of Spades)*

Everything happens for a reason. People who cross our life path do so for a very special reason. The majority of these people offer us some type of direction and encouragement, but others come into our lives to serve as a reflective experience in order to help us to grow spiritually. Even seemingly unpleasant people can offer us very valuable insight into our own soul's journey. Remember, your meeting this person may not necessarily be only for your own benefit, inasmuch as you are most assuredly assisting them on their journey, which is for his/her benefit.

You intuited this card in the Black Suit because tolerance (or the lack thereof) is currently an issue in your life. Perhaps you are being tested spiritually by having a person who you find intolerable being put in your life-path. Try to look beyond the obvious and go deep into the wound. Try to find out the message the Universe is trying to send to you by placing you in the experience which has called this situation up, or has allowed this particular person to come into your life.

Another aspect to consider, of course, is the fact that it very well could be the case that you have been less than tolerant to a fellow journeyer and are being reminded by your guides that you need to be more flexible in your judgment or opinions of others. As the old saying goes, "Until you have walked a mile in my shoes, don't judge me." So goes our own life's journey.

Finally, look within to see if perhaps your own behavior has been testing the tolerance level of those around you. Mountains are always clearer from the plain—stand back a bit and observe your own being and interactions with others. Often we are so entwined in our lives that we fail to take note of how our actions are affecting those around us.

Take a moment to survey your relationships, acquaintances, family and friends to reflect positively on how tolerable you are to others.

Healing Intention

"I accept others as they are in order to be a tolerant person. I tolerate others who could use a tolerant attitude. I conduct myself in a balanced way in order that others will be lovingly tolerant of me, my ideas, my beliefs and my attitudes. I only tolerate those who are searching with a pure heart and who are not hurting and harming others whom they meet on their journey. I offer this intention with love and healing."

Reflective Questions for your Self-Healing

-Why did I choose the card in the position I did?
-What lesson can be learned by focusing on this card?
-How do I interpret the meaning of this card?
-Why is this card significant to me at this moment?

Truth

Truth resonates differently in each and every one of us. What might be regarded as a "truth" for one may not have the same meaning for another. It is important to view truth, and the meaning it has for you, openly and with flexibility. Truth has many forms, all of which have validity. The best way to distinguish clearly between valid and false truth is to follow the intuition associated with it from within you. One may profess outwardly to believe in a "spiritual" or "life" truth, but inwardly is full of doubt and indecision. The way we act on the outside to others is often different from how we reason on the inside with ourselves.

You, and only you, can distinguish for yourself what truth means. The intuition that you feel to the depths of your soul in relation to a particular idea, belief, or opinion is most likely your "truth." Beware, however, that you do not mistake truth which is pure and non-judgmental with a false notion of what you think is a truth, but which, in fact, is rooted in fear, anger, and hatred.

<u>Red Suit</u> *(Ten of Diamonds)*

God, with great wisdom and all-knowing foresight, gave us mortals the ability to reason and to distinguish from an internal perspective what embodies truth and what does not. There are many types of "truths": spiritual truths, life truths, universal truths, intellectual truths, scientific truths, emotional truths, natural truths, and physical truths. Each set contains specific criteria that reflect the broader, more powerful understanding and feeling of truth. We are blessed in that we are given free will in order to decide for ourselves what type of "truth" is resonating the strongest within us—and how we will pursue, develop, and foster this truth.

You intuited this card in the Red Suit because on a soul level you intuitively know and understand truth and what it means to you and your life; or you are well on your way to finding the truths you instinctively search for because it is a part of your soul's desire to do so.

The ability to know "truth" which is pure and full of light is truly a blessing. It gives one the peace of mind needed to continue confidently and without fear on this life's journey, searching even further for the ultimate truths of life and Spirit. Follow your beacon of truth, dear journeyer, and help to light the way for others by shining your truthful knowledge brightly.

Black Suit *(Ten of Spades)*

"Truth" which is absolutely, unequivocally true can be hard to swallow for some journeyers whose paths are not ready to receive it. It is hard to face the cold, hard truth of life and Spirit if one is not spiritually or emotionally ready to handle what God has planned.

The time has come for you to face your truths with an open mind and an honest heart. Intuiting this card in the Black Suit signals that you are ready (on some level) to face issues which you have been avoiding and denying. You are having difficulty in accepting the truths you intuitively know to be true. Your outward struggle is either based on fear, confusion, or a lack of understanding of what you know to be true from an internal vantage point. Confront, accept and in the process, conquer.

Old habits die hard, and living a life that denies the truth you know to be genuine causes stress and hardship for your persona on all levels. Release the earthly bond you have to following a path, which you know, does not lead to the "truth" as God wants, and embrace what you feel in your heart to be the universal truth of life and Spirit.

Healing Intention

"I lovingly search and embrace the universal truths of life and Spirit with an open heart to allow God to guide me toward achieving my soul's purpose and to find the truth that I intuitively seek. I offer this intention with love and healing."

Reflective Questions for your Self-Healing

-Why did I choose the card in the position I did?
-What lesson can be learned from focusing on this card?
-How do I interpret the meaning of this card?
-Why is this card significant to me at this moment?

Understanding

Being an *understanding* person who is sympathetic, tolerant, and wise in either an attitude or in the treatment toward another person is an enviable trait to have. We all could use a little understanding from time to time from another who may not readily agree with our choices. Allowing yourself to be understanding of another person, or to have an understanding of another's situation or condition in this life, will further you along in understanding your own personal life-goals. No one is perfect and part of learning life's lessons is to experience the hardships which occur from making mistakes.

Understanding is not necessarily "condoning" another's choices in life; it is, however, being tolerant and accepting of these choices. Often we may not agree with someone else's life-style, spiritual path or relationship choices, but we are not here to judge them. Only they can do that, from within, for themselves.

As long as your understanding of another does not compromise your own morals or ideals in how you lead *your* life, it is best to be sympathetic and tolerant toward your brothers and sisters. They may desperately need an understanding ear, or an understanding attitude, in order to allow them the opportunity to experience their own self-discovery on their own terms and in their own time frame. No matter how tempting it is to meddle, part of life's lessons is best learned by making mistakes. It is this process that helps us to learn and enables us to proceed accordingly on our own journey.

Red Suit *(Jack of Diamonds)*

Sympathy and tolerance are two very similar attitudes related to understanding. Actually, both of these insightful words can be used to define "understanding." Your selection of this card demonstrates that you are progressing quite nicely on your journey. Being understanding and having an understanding ear or attitude is necessary in allowing yourself to move forward on your life's journey. From this type of understanding, compassion is born. Being sympathetic, in a compassionate, understanding manner cleanses your soul and lifts your heart higher and higher.

Concentrate deeply on this card to intuit the person or relationship, situation, or area of your life in which you have offered, from the purity of your heart, understanding. Once it becomes clear, focus on this image in order to cement it into your psyche. Refer back to this "understanding" anytime you feel the need for a lift. Having understanding, which is compassionate and tolerant, always lifts the spirit and soul. Soar, my friend, soar!

Black Suit *(Jack of Spades)*

Relationships can be like mirrors—they reflect back to you what you give. This card in the Black Suit may be suggesting that you are feeling as though people aren't offering you a sufficient amount of leeway in the "understanding" department. Perhaps people have been critical of your behavior or attitude (one which is very important to you, but goes against their sense of "understanding"). Remember, the attitudes and feelings of others toward you present themselves precipitously in order to allow self-reflection.

Have you been sufficiently understanding of the needs, beliefs, opinions, or attitudes of others? What goes around comes around. It is vitally important to *be* understanding of others, in order for others to *be* understanding of you. This is a two-way street, which many people like to think of as only being one-way. You must give in order to receive.

The fact that you intuited this card in this position is an indication that you perhaps have not been as understanding as you could be. Take this time to reflect upon your daily relationships with family, friends and colleagues in order to pull out the blockage, which is hindering your understanding of others, or their understanding of you. Something is not allowing you and your interactions the capacity to understand lovingly and unconditionally. By removing this obstacle, you can then proceed more confidently on your journey with a sense of understanding borne out of compassion and tolerance. In turn, others will be more apt to offer you the understanding you need.

Healing Intention

"I offer an understanding ear and attitude toward my fellow human beings in order that they may in turn be understanding of me and my needs. My understanding is compassionate, sympathetic and wise, without ulterior motive and from the pureness of my heart. I offer this intention with love and healing."

Reflective Questions for your Self-Healing

-Why did I choose the card in the position I did?
-What lesson can be learned by focusing on this card?
-How do I interpret the meaning of this card?
-Why is this card significant to me at this moment?

Worthiness

So often, perhaps too often, people question their *worthiness* regarding whether they are deserving, are a good member of society, or are fulfilling their spiritual destiny properly. What is worthiness? Simply, it is the state of having sufficient merit or value. God did not create us to be unworthy, hence we are not undeserving. We are created to enjoy and relish in the abundance which is available to us from the Universe.

Anytime someone you love dearly or just know casually utters the words "I'm not worthy," it should make you pause with a sense of compassion for that person. Making such a negative, untrue statement is damaging, not only to that person's proper place in society, but also in the Universe. This way of thinking must be reversed and changed to reflect a deserving attitude, which is worthy of all that Spirit has to offer—not just to some of us in this life, but to all of us.

Allow yourself, and encourage others, to enjoy all that is worthy and inalienably ours. Possessing a sense of worthiness is not a privilege reserved for a few. It is the right of all.

Red Suit *(Queen of Diamonds)*

This card, in the Red Suit position, may be a gentle reminder to you to take note that you are a worthy person. Often, people go about their daily routine without taking the time to realize this simple truth. Focus your loving energy on this word and concentrate on its meaning—having merit and value in a deserving way. Allow yourself the luxury to bask in the worthiness of your being and essence.

After all, having a sense of worthiness enhances a person's self-esteem, gives one more confidence, and allows a feeling of doing some good for oneself. You intuited this card because, on some level, you completed a self-awareness process that is directly related to your own self-worth (or in recognizing the worthiness of someone else). Now, all you have to do is rejoice in your self-worth or the worthiness of another by taking the time to recognize it fully and clearly. Go ahead…do it! You are worthy!

Black Suit *(Queen of Spades)*

At times, one can put too much emphasis on one's self-worth, which conveys to others an attitude of superiority or arrogance. While it is necessary to recognize your own worthiness, it is equally important to do so with a sense of balance and honesty. Flaunting your "value and merit" in an intimidating manner is not done with purity of motive. Trying to impress others with your own sense of worthiness is not done so in a loving and healing manner. People will be impressed naturally and without force—they do not need to be told to because it will be obvious. It is important for you to survey your recent interactions with others and the motives behind your actions, in order to see clearly the reason why you selected this card in the Black Suit position.

In contrast, this card could be signaling to you to take note of your own attitude towards your own self-worth. Have you been generating negative vibrations by questioning your own self-worth? Do you feel unworthy? If so, ask yourself why? In order to reverse this type of negative cycle, it is necessary to concentrate on the positive and to recognize consciously the worthiness that is uniquely yours.

Finally, perhaps the Universe is trying to remind you that you have neglected to recognize the worthiness of others with whom you come into contact. It is important to treat others in the same manner in which you wish to be treated. Recognizing the worthiness of a fellow being is important not only to him/her, but it is also important to you and to your place in the Universe.

Only you know for sure the reason or action that prompted the selection of this card. Search for it from within, then face it with either humility for being too assertive with others (regarding your own sense of self-worth or by not recognizing theirs); or with pride because you have great self-worth but have neglected to recognize it and let it flourish, as it should.

Healing Intention

"I am worthy. I am deserving. I accept my own God-given right to worthiness with purity of motive and without pretense. As well, I recognize the personal and spiritual worth of others. I offer this intention with love and healing."

Reflective Questions for your Self-Healing

-Why did I choose the card in the position I did?
-What lesson can be learned by focusing on this card?
-How do I interpret the meaning of this card?
-Why is this card significant to me at this moment?

Zest

Words people use to define *zest* include enthusiasm, interest, eagerness and energy. This exhilarating word can both empower and excite a person at the same time! Having zest is an attribute that will spread quickly to others. It is an energy-enhancing word that will energize you at the mere mention of it.

A popular vernacular phrase used in everyday speech refers to a person having a "zest for life." This is a condition that every man, woman and child should be experiencing at every possible moment. Life is precious and should be enjoyed fully. Putting zest into all that you do will make a positive and profound difference in your attitude, actions, interactions and life-purpose. Living zestfully will naturally allow you to live positively. Good energy begets good energy, which means that zest produces even more zest.

<u>Red Suit</u> *(King of Diamonds)*

Living our lives fully, the way we are meant to, is a remarkable achievement. Modern-day life tends to throw monkey wrenches into our pursuit of happiness. These obstacles prevent us from following our hearts to enjoy life to its fullest potential.

You, zesty journeyer, do take the necessary time to live zestfully, or at least have recently begun to do so. Life is a series of ups and downs. The trick is to pass over the low points, and ride the high points for as long as you can. Enjoying the high points with a feeling of zest will allow you to maximize this sensation. This effervescent sensation will repeat itself over and over as long as you are willing to allow it. Zestfully and enthusiastically enjoy all that the Universe puts before you.

Recently, or continually, you have harnessed a sense of zest in your life. Continue to enjoy life to its fullest. If you are unsure as to what zesty part of your life this card refers, meditate upon this word for several minutes to image in your mind's eye all the areas of your life that are full of zest. Heck, why not stick this card in your pocket to remind you all day about the zest you have in your life.

Black Suit *(King of Spades)*

Sometimes the more negative aspects of our life journey can invade our psyche and firmly plant themselves into our thoughts. When this happens, it is vital that each aspect be viewed from a positive perspective in order to reverse this damaging cycle. After all, every negative situation has positive points. It may be difficult to focus on the positive aspects at a time when you are consumed only with the negative; reach deep within to pull out the positive energy, which is engulfed in the negative.

Life-dramas can preoccupy our thoughts and actions to the point where we find ourselves in a deep rut that is mundane or full of despair, and seems impossible to crawl out of. This is neither interesting nor enriching on any level—mentally, physically, emotionally, and certainly not spiritually. You intuited this card in this position because you have a situation in your life that is pulling you down by zapping your positive energy. Whether it is a partner, family member, work colleague or work circumstance, or a personal predicament, you are wallowing in a pigsty of negativity. Left untouched, it will eventually suck you dry of all your life-enhancing, universal life-force energy.

Think deeply and honestly about a person or situation, which is impeding you from enjoying zest in either an aspect, or in your entire life, by draining you of the will to enjoy life fully. You need to reverse this cycle by releasing the negativity surrounding this person or situation. This could be through forgiveness, or a promise to move on from a past injustice done upon you. This life is too short to live in a fog of despair, guilt, or fear. Release, my friend, and find in your heart the place where you are able to enjoy once again the abundance of life that is filled with joy and zest—the life the Universe entitles you to and means for you to live.

Healing Intention

"I live life with zest, enjoying all that the Universe has to offer me. I wish that others may observe my zest for life and hence be encouraged and strengthened to consciously put zest into their lives. I offer this intention with love and healing."

Reflective Questions for your Self-Healing

-Why did I choose the card in the position I did?
-What lesson can be learned by focusing on this card?
-How do I interpret the meaning of this card?
-Why is this card significant to me at this moment?

About the Author

Todd Jay Leonard's life journey has taken him to the far reaches of the world where he has studied, taught, researched, traveled and worked in North and South America, Europe, Africa, Australia and Asia.

An ordained minister and university professor, Reverend Leonard has actively sought out spiritual knowledge from the time he was a child. He has studied religion formally, and as a hobby, for most of his life. The importance he now places upon self-awakening and self-healing has its roots in the energy-based therapy of *Reiki*. Trained in the *Usui Shiki Ryoho* System of *Reiki*, he is a Master-Teacher, offering this energy-based laying-of-hands healing treatment in Japan, where he lives, teaches, and writes.

Professor Leonard lectures internationally on education, comparative culture, and spiritually-based topics; also, he has published extensively in academic journals, magazines, and newspapers in the areas of cross-cultural understanding, Teaching English as a Foreign Language (TEFL), and religious studies.

His publications include *Crossing Cultures: America and Japan* (Kenkyusha, 1992); *Extra! Extra! Read All About It!* (Kinseido, 1994); *Team-Teaching Together: A Bilingual Resource Handbook for JTEs and AETs* (Taishukan, 1994); *Talk, Talk: American-Style* (Macmillan Languagehouse, 1996); *Words to Write By: Developing Writing Skills through Quotations* (Macmillan Languagehouse, 1997); *The Better Half: Exploring the Changing Roles of Men and Women with Current Newspaper Articles* (Macmillan Languagehouse, 1997); *East Meets West: An American in Japan* (Kenkyusha, 1998); *East Meets West: Problems and Solutions—Understanding Misunderstandings between JTEs and ALTs* (Taishukan, 1999); *Trendy Traditions: A Cross Cultural Skills-Based Reader of Essays on the United States* (Macmillan Languagehouse, 2002); *Business as Usual: An Integrated Approach to Learning English* (Seibido, 2003); and *Letters Home: Musings of an American Expatriate Living in Japan* (iUniverse, 2003).

0-595-29331-X

CPSIA information can be obtained
at www.ICGtesting.com
Printed in the USA
FFOW01n1844211015
17904FF

9 780595 293315